Prophet and Loss

"An exhausting challenge of pastoring is carrying the weight of leadership while experiencing personal loss. You must shepherd through the pain when it comes. How can you do so in a healthy way? In *Prophet and Loss*, David Woolverton writes an excellent guide for church leaders who want to understand how God redeems grief for his purposes. This book will lighten the load for many who feel the weight of grief."

—SAM RAINER, president, Church Answers

"*Prophet and Loss* challenges me to think in new ways about leadership. With his characteristic candor, humor, and humility, David Woolverton draws from personal experience and from the lives of biblical prophets to dissect the critical roles of grief and loss in the leader's journey. This book will inspire you to lead, but not before first requiring you to take a hard look in the mirror, to make a realistic appraisal of what likely lies ahead, and to prepare for some wrestling."

—ROB SKACEL, founder, True Edge Performance Solutions

"David Woolverton's *Prophet and Loss* is a unique and powerful exploration, if not personal examination, on grief in one's life and organization. It is both honest and hopeful as it encourages the leader to navigate the contours of loss wisely and intentionally. Through the lens of Jesus and the prophets, he unpacks how to embrace grief in a way that nurtures healing and more authentic leadership."

—KEVIN GUSHIKEN, director of PhD in leadership program, Lancaster Bible College

"This important book, so full of insight, wisdom, and tenderness, will help leaders develop a broader theology of grief, a greater appreciation for the biblical prophets and their function among us today, and possibly do more to realign our mission to reach others for the gospel of Christ than just about anything I can personally think of."

—ALISA BAIR, author of *Grief Is a Dancer*

"I am grateful for this book and for Pastor David Woolverton's willingness to reflect on the most painful organizational losses from a grounded perspective of faith, hope, and love to equip organizational expansion. His creative imagination of the prophetic journey and his great love for Jesus embolden readers to take heart that when they grieve, they are walking in prophetic heritage and are never forsaken in the unfolding plan for us within the kingdom of God."

—DUSTIN RISSER, author of *Creativity, Theology, and Posttraumatic Growth: The Sacred Impulse of Play and Transformation out of Tragedy*

"In *Prophet and Loss*, David Woolverton masterfully addresses the deeply complex topic of dealing personally with, as well as leading others through, the life-altering impact of grief. With the goal of helping leaders lead their people and organizations through change and loss, he dives deeply into this sometimes overlooked, or intentionally avoided, challenge. The daunting task of walking and leading through grief, though never easy, is infused with encouraging wisdom and hope in this wonderfully perceptive book."

—MICHAEL CHRISTIAN SHAW, author of *Faithful Are the Wounds: A Memoir*

"In 2 Corinthians 4:7, Paul writes, 'We have this treasure in jars of clay' (ESV). As we live the wonderful life and work that the Lord has given us, we can forget that the great treasure which we steward is housed in 'jars of clay'—jars that quickly and easily become chipped, cracked, and broken. With a fresh measure of authenticity and humanity, David Woolverton enables us to look at those broken and bruised places without judgment and find the treasure in it all."

—KEVIN ESHLEMAN, senior pastor, Ephrata Community Church

"It was with gratitude and eager expectation I received this book from my friend David Woolverton. His life experiences with grief as a man of God, pastor, theologian, professor, and leadership coach have placed him in a position of authority to address this important issue. Through the wisdom and insights given in this book, you will discover as I have, how grief is a gift of grace for the transitions and loss we all face in life."
—WESLEY SIEGRIST, executive pastor of operations, Ephrata Community Church

"*Prophet and Loss* is a remarkable journey that brings together the wonderful stories of Scripture and David's authentic experiences with grief. These stories and insights are beautifully woven together to help the pastor, minister, and everyday follower of Christ consider what it means to walk through grief alongside others while holding the hand of Christ who meets us there. I cried, I healed, I came out better equipped to meet others in their grief, and I was able to process my own grief. This a must-read for all."
—HEATHER HENSON, affiliate professor of pastoral ministries, Kairos University

"In this time when we are experiencing a global outbreak of grief, David Woolverton wisely encourages us as individuals and leaders to face the grief head on. He reminds us, 'Our losses are the arenas within which genuine spiritual growth occurs.' Prepare to be moved, inspired, and forever changed by this transformative literary masterpiece."
—DON EISENHAUER, founder, Coaching at End of Life

Prophet and Loss

Embracing Grief, Nurturing Resilience, and Harnessing Authentic Leadership

DAVID E. WOOLVERTON

WIPF & STOCK · Eugene, Oregon

PROPHET AND LOSS
Embracing Grief, Nurturing Resilience, and Harnessing Authentic Leadership

Copyright © 2024 David E. Woolverton. All rights reserved. Except for brief quotations in critical publications or reviews, no part of this book may be reproduced in any manner without prior written permission from the publisher. Write: Permissions, Wipf and Stock Publishers, 199 W. 8th Ave., Suite 3, Eugene, OR 97401.

Wipf & Stock
An Imprint of Wipf and Stock Publishers
199 W. 8th Ave., Suite 3
Eugene, OR 97401

www.wipfandstock.com

PAPERBACK ISBN: 979-8-3852-0815-9
HARDCOVER ISBN: 979-8-3852-0816-6
EBOOK ISBN: 979-8-3852-0817-3

02/06/24

All Scripture quotations, unless otherwise indicated, are from the New Revised Standard Version Bible, copyright © 1989 National Council of the Churches of Christ in the United States of America. Used by permission. All rights reserved worldwide.

Scripture quotations marked CJB are taken from the Complete Jewish Bible by David H. Stern. Copyright © 1998. All rights reserved. Used by permission of Messianic Jewish Publishers, 6120 Day Long Lane, Clarksville, MD 21029. www.messianicjewish.net.

*To Rita and Paul, my mom and dad,
who, as they faced into death,
taught me how to live by faith.*

Contents

	Acknowledgments	ix
	Introduction	1
	A Prophet in Time: Jeremiah	17
1	Denial	23
	A Prophet in Time: Anna	48
2	Anger	55
	A Prophet in Time: Hannah	75
3	Bargaining	81
	A Prophet in Time: Huldah	104
4	Depression	109
	A Prophet in Time: Hosea	149
5	Acceptance	157
	Epilogue	171
	Appendix: Building a Mosaic—A Group Exercise	177
	Works Consulted	179

Acknowledgments

ON DECEMBER 22, 2022, two days before Christmas Eve, I tested positive for COVID-19. A pastor's nightmare, for sure, since Christmas Eve is the biggest worship event of most local churches. I rebooted my plans, got another pastor to preach in my place, oriented my worship teams to move on without me, and planted myself in an upstairs bedroom for what became eleven days of quarantine. Almost immediately, it became clear to me that I had to "do something" to prevent myself from going stir crazy from boredom (daytime television and I just do not get along).

So, on day two, I opened a Word document, set my hands on the keyboard, and prayed: "Lord, consecrate me by the blood of Jesus to be a vessel through whom you speak to your people. Holy Spirit, write through my hands the message you want your church to hear." With eyes still closed, I started typing.

Two and a half hours later (now with eyes open), the Jeremiah story had been written. At the time, I had no idea where all of it would lead. By the end of the next day of writing, chapter 1 was complete. Then, the next day I repeated the process—each day offering the same prayer, closing my eyes to start, and emerging with an additional section, story, or chapter having been written. By day eleven, my last day of quarantine, nearly two-thirds of the book was done, a pattern to the writing had emerged, and a platform for *Prophet and Loss* had developed.

Therefore, I must acknowledge, first, the Holy Spirit—for this book would not have been written without his guidance. I'm trusting that its message honors the intent of my prayer. I am humbled by what the Lord placed on my heart to write.

Second, I must thank my gracious wife, Kristine, for making and bringing me my meals on a tray multiple times each day, running the household by herself for the eleven days of my isolation, and encouraging

Acknowledgments

me to keep writing even though she was getting tired of reciting "in sickness and in health" (part of our wedding vows) under her breath each time she took on our stairs with yet another tray of food.

And third, tongue-in-cheek, I thank the coronavirus ultimately for motivating me to spend ten to twelve hours each day writing when I could have been binging on reruns of *The West Wing* (okay, I did do some of that), *Star Trek*, or *Gilligan's Island*.

I also want to thank Matt Wimer, managing editor at Wipf and Stock, Christopher Klimkowski, my copy editor, Savanah N. Landerholm, my typesetter, and the wonderful team of editors, marketers, directors, and assistants there—for the incredible partnership they offered me in publishing this book. I so appreciated the well-laid-out process for moving my manuscript to book form, the ongoing coaching and encouragement, and even the flexible deadlines designed to keep me motivated but not overwhelmed. What a solidly good and gracious team.

Finally, I have so much appreciation for the many people over the years who have entrusted me with their losses, their pain, their grief, their prayers, and their hope. Each of their situations of loss changed me—forcing me to face my way-too-often naive understanding of the God who gives and the God who takes away (Job 1:21). For each of their losses, as well as the hope that continues to emerge from them, I am truly grateful.

Introduction

I REALLY HAD NO idea what I was doing.

I was a pastor, after all, not an entrepreneur. In fact, I was a pastor in a church that was growing quite rapidly. We had made decisions to intentionally reach out to the unchurched and, in fact, indeed they were coming in droves.

It was 1998 and the congregation I was serving had grown from the three hundred or so in worship attendance ten years prior to well over twelve hundred. Each year, it seemed like we were adding at least another hundred new members. Because of the rapid growth, my job description had changed multiple times—landing, out of necessity, on the role of overseeing congregational care.

As more and more people came and were being impacted by the gospel, more and more of those people were seeking counseling on a variety of issues as they sought to reorient their lives according to their deepening spiritual formation. The growing demand on my time to provide what I called "triage"—listening to the primary issues presented and then referring them to appropriate counselors in the area—became overwhelming. I had made a point back then to never refer anyone from my congregation to any counselor that I had not vetted personally. And I had vetted quite a few licensed counselors who had a strong faith perspective. Yet, after several years of referring to these counselors, their available times became waiting lists, and the waiting lists were often three or more months behind the needs. I did what I could, often adding to the triage sessions to help those people sufficiently cope with whatever crisis they were facing until they could see the counselor. I was simply overwhelmed . . . and overworked, as my schedule went from forty to fifty and then sixty work hours per week.

Have you ever been there—overworked, yet passionate about what you were called to do?

In praying through this, I remember saying to God, "These people are hurting, Lord. Show me what to do. I just can't keep up this schedule."

After a very difficult day, I began my evening devotions with a simple prayer: "Lord, what do you want me to do?" My devotional reading that day was from Mark 6 and the account of the feeding of the five thousand. As I read through the text, I resonated with the disciples when they went to Jesus and implored him to "send the crowd away" so that they could buy something to eat (Mark 6:36). They too, I imagined, had compassion for the people, but were also a bit overwhelmed by the sheer volume of their needs.

Then I read verse 37—"But he answered them, 'You give them something to eat.'" I wanted to move on quickly in my reading, but I couldn't get past that phrase. In fact, the very first word—*you*—seemed to hang in the air. The Lord couldn't possibly be telling me to minister to these people myself, could he? I was already overwhelmed. "Lord, what are you saying to me?"

GOD'S BOLD ASK

In prayer, I heard the voice of the Holy Spirit speak an idea: "Open a counseling center." It was as clear a message as I had ever heard. I knew, absolutely knew, that I was being directed to do this.

I also knew that I felt so out of my comfort zone in listening to that voice.

I had no idea how to begin, so I did two things rather quickly. First, I asked a small group of people from my congregation to form a "dream team" with me for the purpose of researching and discerning whether such a center was viable, and if so, to develop a marketing plan; and second, I developed a list of about sixty to seventy church pastors in the area and personally called them to see if it would help their ministry if there was a Christ-centered counseling center in the area, and if so, would they commit to referring to us. I don't think I had a single negative response.

The team formed rather quickly. Our research took over two years to complete—demographic studies, gathering information on marketing strategies, discussing types of counseling services we would provide, as well as the limitations and liabilities that would come with operating a not-for-profit counseling center, something we felt called to be. By the time we had finished collecting and collating all the necessary information, it became clear that the center was really needed within our community. Each of the dream team members was solidly in favor of us moving forward.

At the time, there were no other faith-based counseling centers in our immediate area. So, we finalized our marketing plan, filled out the paperwork to establish ourselves as a 501(c)(3) nonprofit corporation, formed a board of directors by adding a few persons to the dream team, and set out to execute our plan. We just needed the right organizational name that would communicate the heart of our center.

POWER IN THE NAME

It was on a church staff retreat soon afterward that my dear friend and colleague, Alisa Bair, unknowingly provided what we needed. She was doing her private devotions in a corner of the retreat lodge as I walked by. She called me over, handed me her Bible, and said, "David, the Lord gave me this verse for you. Read it." It was Jer 6:16—"Thus says the Lord: Stand at the crossroads, and look, and ask for the ancient paths, where the good way lies; and walk in it and find rest for your souls." I immediately knew in my spirit that the Lord was speaking yet again. I had been looking for guidance as to the overall framework of the center, a "mission" that would direct us, along with the perfect name that would identify us by that mission. This verse provided all of that.

In our planning, we had felt that the Lord was leading us to become a mission-focused organization that would provide high quality, Christ-centered counseling services specifically to the underserved and economically challenged population in the western portion of our county, where faith-based counseling services were quite limited. We wanted to help people reconnect to the One who would give them the "rest" that they were looking for, a connection to the "ancient paths" of God's wisdom, and to make it affordable and accessible. Based on the Jeremiah passage, we took on the name Crossroads Counseling Center. Jeremiah 6:16 became our "theme verse" as well as our accountability plumb line. We were ready to launch.

FOUR PROBLEMS

We just had four problems—we had no location, no money, no counselors, and no clients. Providentially, because our church had grown so quickly, the leaders previously had asked my wife and I to take a housing allowance so that they could convert the parsonage where we lived into office spaces. I did not realize at the time that my once master bedroom eventually would become my new converted office, as the parsonage was reoriented into the congregational care department. I remembered thinking that the parsonage/congregational care offices would make the perfect location for the center. A shared space. We simply needed to obtain permission from the church leaders and negotiate a "cost-efficient" (i.e., hopefully free) rental agreement.

In terms of counselors, God provided there as well. One of the center's board members was a pharmacist. It seemed as if every day a client would come in to fill a prescription who the pharmacist happened to know was a professional counselor. He would share the mission behind what we were doing and by the time they exited the pharmacy, they had agreed to meet with me for a vision-casting lunch. One by one, they agreed to join our team—amazingly for a fraction of the fee they most likely would have received in the public sector.

We also needed money to underwrite the cost of services for those who were in our target demographic and unable to pay the full price of services—namely, people who were economically challenged. We needed benefactors.

So, I went to the leaders of the congregation I served as a starting point and asked if they would support us financially. One of the center's board members and I presented our marketing plan and our well-researched strategy. We had charts. We had slides. We had an amazing presentation.

The board said no. Ouch.

They did not feel that it was wise for them to take on such a cost within the congregational budget, nor did they want to assume liability for a counseling center. I remember feeling defeated by their decision, ready to give up. By this point, we had put well over several years of research and countless hours into the design of this center.

Yet, in that moment, something stirred in me. The phrase "stand at the crossroads" kept repeating in my mind. I opened my mouth and found myself asking what must have sounded like an impertinent question: "Would you support the concept of the center, and allow us to share space in the parsonage, if I raised the money apart from the budget?"

I'm sure they were not trying to be insensitive or mean, but several of the leaders laughed at that question. Accurately or not, I interpreted the laughter to mean, "I don't think Dave realizes how much money he has to raise or exactly what he's getting himself into." Finally, the chairperson said, "Pastor Dave, sure, if you can raise the money apart from the budget—and not pull from the resources that normally would be given to the church—then yes, I think we'd all agree to support this." They moved on with their next item of business as the other presenter and I packed up our materials and exited the room.

POSITIONED FOR CRISIS

For some strange reason, I left that meeting excited by the challenge. As I shared this information with the rest of the center's board of directors, they came up with the idea of doing a fundraising banquet. We set a date in May 2003, booked a banquet hall, secured the money to cover the cost of the banquet through donations from the board of directors, and invited just about everyone we could think of that might have a heart for what we were doing and the resources to help.

Just as everything was in motion, I received word from my district superintendent that I was to be transferred to a new church as of July 1. The good news about that move was that I would still be in the area. It was a church in crisis—a congregation that was dealing with significant conflict. Since my district superintendent knew that I was doing my doctoral work in conflict leadership, I got pegged for the position. The prospects of the new role actually excited me. The challenge was that I would now need to split my focus three ways: my current pastoral role (since I still had about five more months before the transition), which was still running me at about sixty hours per week; the counseling center's formation; and the transitioning process of exiting one church and starting at a new one.

The fundraising event was amazing. Over a hundred people came that evening. I had a few individuals for whom I had offered counseling support ask if they could help by sharing their testimony at the banquet. Doing so brought tangible examples to bear on the vision we were casting. Then came my simple invitation for partnership—asking that if anyone was inclined to give to the center's mission that it not impact their normal tithe to their local church.

That night we raised $250,000 in pledged support to be given over five years. In turn, the church allowed us to "rent" the parsonage/office wing by providing vouchers for counseling equal to what a fair rental value would have cost. They would even renovate the rooms to make them accessible and private for the intended use. We opened the center officially Sunday, June 1, 2003, one day prior to my last day at the church.

A little over one year later, I had a heart attack.

FACING DEATH TO FIND LIFE

"You're an enigma." The cardiologist on-call in the emergency room that night was deadpan, making it difficult for me to read his body language. It was about three o'clock in the morning by the time he had come into my room. He wore the classic long white medical jacket over shirt, tie, and slacks. He struck me as being someone with many years of experience, slightly graying and sufficiently stoic, yet without being aloof or uncaring.

Life looks different from a hospital bed. Perhaps you know exactly what I mean.

It was Saturday night, July 3, 2004. My wife, Kristine, and I had returned a few days prior from one of the most relaxing vacations we've ever had—spending time reading and relaxing at Lake Placid in upstate New York. Upon returning, I received word of the tragic death of one my good friends. We had made it home in time for her funeral. The evening after the funeral, I started to feel like I had the flu, so I spent the next three days in bed. On the third night, my heart started going into an arrhythmia.

In my clinical training years earlier, I had worked numerous holiday shifts in the emergency departments and trauma bays. It was always chaotic. I did not relish the idea of being a patient in one this weekend, but at the insistent advice of my primary care doctor (who was also my friend), Kristine drove me in. We arrived about 11:30 p.m. They immediately took me back and began to triage me based on my symptoms. I ended up in a room, hooked up to a bunch of heart monitor leads, blood pressure cuff, and an IV drip. Various nurses and the ED attending came in and out, taking blood, checking vitals, printing off EKG reports, well into the early morning hours. The cardiologist on call reviewed all the information prior to entering, adding fuel to his "enigma" comment.

"Under normal circumstances, I would take that as a compliment," I retorted, rather anxiously, but exercising my humor as a cover to my fear (a typical trait of mine). "What do you mean?"

"All of your test results are coming back normal except for one. Your troponin level is fifty."

"What should it be?" I asked.

"Zero. So, something is going on with you, but we're just not sure what." I think my fever, body aches, and chills were throwing them off their standard trail.

Introduction

"What do you think it could be?" The doctor immediately started rattling off a list of possible causes to my symptoms, even counting them off on his fingers. The sheer number of options was overwhelming.

"Look, doc," I interrupted, "I'm a straight shooter. I've worked in emergency rooms, so I get the drill. You're the expert. What do *you* think is going on?"

Without missing a beat, the cardiologist said, "I think you had a heart attack." Again, his deadpan would have made him an amazing poker player.

The effect was real and immediate. Kristine squeezed my hand tightly and I sucked in an unexpected gulp of air. It was a proclamation that was difficult to hear. A heart attack? But I was only 41 years old!

"What would you say if you lied?" My humor was present, but significantly stifled by the audacity of the potential diagnosis.

Finally, the doctor said, "Look, we won't know for sure until we do a cardiac catheterization."

Since it was a holiday weekend, and since I was not classified as an emergency (for which, retrospectively, I am grateful), I had to wait until the following Tuesday morning for that test. When the time for the test came, they prepped me and then rolled me on a gurney to the cath lab. There was another patient still being worked on, so the transport person parked my gurney in the hallway outside the lab and walked away. I was totally alone in the hallway with nothing to do other than to engage my thoughts and the God whom I have served in ministry for the prior fifteen years. In prayer, I began a conversation with the Almighty.

A FAMILIAR VOICE

"Lord? What 'cha doin'?" (I don't know about you, but I'm an Italian kid from New Jersey. This is the way I talk with God sometimes.)

Even in that moment of my fear, I was not prone to ask, "Why me?" For most of my ministry up to that point, I had been in situations that had pushed that inquiry button numerous times, the responses of which had shaped my character and deepened my appreciation that being a follower of Jesus does not make me immune to the harsh realities and limitations of being human. I thought my question was fair, though, wondering how this scenario was playing out within the ongoing arena of my call.

"Did I call you to ministry?" The Voice was almost immediate in response, gentle and yet direct, expecting an answer.

"Absolutely," I replied, out loud, my response echoing in the hallway. I thoroughly felt confident in that answer.

"Did I gift you for ministry?"

"Absolutely." Again, I was confident, and I felt good about my response.

"Do you trust me?"

That third question hung in the air for what was, most likely, just a minute, but which felt more like ten. During that span of time, I remember thinking of all the times that God had been faithful to me, how the Lord had provided within situations where I had struggled, how God had poured out amazing grace in and through the ministry situations I was a part of over the years, and how God had never, ever, abandoned me—even in my times of rebellion. Mental pictures of God's faithfulness, of God's love, lavished on me in so many ways flooded my mind causing me to tear up with gratefulness.

"Absolutely," I replied, more quietly than before, yet confident in God's grace, even if not with my circumstances. "I trust you."

"Then why are you worried?" It was a simple question. Yet, I sensed that it was more declaration than anything else. My response was heartfelt praise. Right there in the vacant hallway, tears running down my cheeks, I started to sing—out loud—praise choruses, verses of hymns, whatever came to mind.

It may have been the Valium that they gave me, but as the nurse came out to wheel me into the cath lab, I was overwhelmed by that peace that "surpasses all understanding" that Paul wrote about in Phil 4:7. I just knew that everything was going to be okay, no matter what.

When the cardiologist was ready to start, he indicated to the anesthesiologist to begin the IV that would make me sleepy for the procedure. I interrupted him and asked that I be allowed to stay awake throughout.

"In fact," I asked, "can you please talk me through every part of what you're doing and what you're seeing. I'm very much okay with it all."

The doctor was great. He turned the monitor so that I could see what he was seeing as he extended the catheter through an artery in my groin and up into my heart. I saw my heart from an entirely different perspective that day.

"Ah, there it is," the doctor said. "There . . . do you see? You have a completely blocked artery in the lower portion of your heart." He pointed to the monitor, to the specific source of my issue. "But look here . . . see this?" he said, again pointing to something his trained eyes were discerning, but mine could not make out. "There are two collateral arteries that have bypassed the blocked artery. That's why it was confusing us. Okay, we're done here." He started to finish up his work, withdrawing the catheter and indicating to his team that they were finished.

"Wait," I said. "Aren't you going to do angioplasty? Don't I need a stent in that artery?"

"Not at all," he replied. "Why would we do what your heart already did?"

"No!" I stated strongly, pointing my finger up at him. "*God* did this! *God* did this!"

I couldn't see his mouth since he was masked, but I could tell that the doctor's eyes smiled as he moved away from the table, allowing the nurse to apply pressure to my recently punctured artery. I knew God had done something amazing.

I just didn't realize how amazing until several weeks later.

A NEW MISSION

I took the next three weeks off to recover. New medicines were prescribed, as well as a new diet and a new commitment to reduce stress. On the Saturday before my first Sunday back in the pulpit, at about three o'clock in the morning, God woke me up. Literally. I was sound asleep when what felt like a hand shook my shoulder. Waking up, I thought Kristine was nudging me to stop snoring, but she was rolled over facing the other side of the bed.

Have you ever felt God wake you up in the middle of the night?

Now awake, I heard that familiar Voice again. "Get up and pray." It was clear and insistent.

Getting out of bed, I quietly moved to one of the chairs we have in the bedroom, sat down and said, "What do you want me to pray about?" It was then that the Lord began to download a life-changing mission.

"Remember that you had a heart attack?"

"Yes, Lord. I most definitely remember that." How could I forget?

"You remember that you had a completely blocked artery, but that two collateral arteries naturally bypassed the blockage?"

"Yes, Lord. I remember."

"David, the heart of my people is blocked—preventing them from connecting with my heart. So much has caused that blockage, but I have created two 'collateral arteries' to bypass that blockage—to reconnect the heart of my people with mine. One is called 'love,' the other is called 'forgiveness.' I want you to preach and teach love and forgiveness to restore what needs to be restored."

I couldn't tell you when it started, but I was now sobbing, tears pouring out of my eyes. Those tears were a mixture of sadness for the condition of God's people, but also such incredible relief that God was somehow making sense out of my heart attack, that God was crafting a greater purpose out of what had been one of the scariest experiences of my life.

I was fully awake now, but I went back to bed and tried to sleep a little longer before the alarm would inaugurate my first day back. I could not. Getting up, I went downstairs and tore up my notes for the sermon I had prepared. That morning, I shared with the congregation the story of my encounter with God, and I began a new mission: to preach and teach love and forgiveness, and to build bridges for people to connect to the heart of the Lord.

To do so, I knew I had to face into my own issues of loss. My heart attack had singularly challenged me, revealing deeper levels of fear and insecurity that, as I reflected, would sneak up at pivotal times in my leadership. I needed to confront what I know now were anxiety reactions of grief—both actual and perceived—so that they would no longer preempt or sabotage my leadership, but rather would inform it as I participated in what God was doing redemptively through it.

Since then, what I began to understand was that organizations rise or fall based on the personal integrity of their leaders—an integrity rooted in honest vulnerability before the God who knows us, who calls us, who equips us, and who sends us.

One of the early lessons I learned was from William Bridges's book, *Managing Transitions: Making the Most of Change*—namely, that for any organization to experience "new beginnings," they would have to go through "endings."[1] To me, that meant that leaders would need to face into their own issues related to grief and loss before they could lead others through it—personally and organizationally.

I knew that God was going to be taking me on a unique journey of connecting people—God's people—to God's greater mission. I had to find both the right mentors and spiritual directors to help me navigate those paths. I found some of them by looking to the biblical prophets—to the ones who had gone before me in this subterranean emotional quest.

This book is a reflection on what I've learned.

---

1. See Bridges and Bridges, *Transitions*. Since I spend quite a bit of time reflecting on these principles in my first book, *Mission Rift*, I won't go into great details in this book.

INTRODUCTION

WHY GRIEF?

In specific terms, grief is one of the primary emotions of change. Certainly, there are other emotions related to change, but after over thirty-five years in ministry, I would argue that grief is the most important. In fact, in my experience, the more significant the change is, the more intense the grief response will be. We are most familiar with grief as it relates to death, and death is certainly one of the more potent arenas for experiencing grief. Yet, grief also comes at other times and in other contexts—both personal as well as professional. I'll explore those too.

In fact, any context that involves change involves grief—whether we acknowledge it or not. Elisabeth Kübler-Ross, clearly the pioneer voice in modern understandings of grief, reflects this understanding. In her book, *Death: The Final Stage of Growth*, she wrote: "The stages of dying that I have described apply equally to any significant change (e.g., retirement, moving to a new city, changing jobs, divorce) in a person's life, and change is a regular occurrence in human existence. If you can face and understand your ultimate death, perhaps you can learn to face and deal productively with each change that presents itself in your life."[2]

My doctorate is in church conflict leadership. The main context of my leadership over the years, therefore, has been the local church, as well as other ministry-related arenas, as I have sought to provide either primary visionary organizational direction, or consultative services to assist pastors and leaders in navigating within and beyond the constructs of conflict. Leaders are catalysts for change. For years, I have led with a very specific axiom: *A catalyst produces change. Change produces transition. Transition produces loss. Loss produces conflict. Always.* A leader, therefore, must have the ability to "navigate their people through the grief that inevitably accompanies change in their organization. Anyone can initiate change. A true movement leader, however, serves as an ambassador for the redemptive work of God's love as it mediates the losses brought about by such change."[3]

Leaders, however, cannot give away what they do not have—a lesson that leadership expert Dr. John C. Maxwell taught me decades ago. Leadership, therefore, requires a solid working theology of grief—its theory and its praxis—both, most ideally, having been learned through the facing of

---

2. Kübler-Ross, *Death: The Final Stage*, 145. Additional resources on this theme include: Jeffreys, *Helping Grieving People*, 19; and Bridges and Bridges, *Transitions*. I adapt the thesis and apply it here to the context of prophetic leadership.

3. Woolverton, *Mission Rift*, 45.

loss personally and professionally. In fact, genuine missional leaders cannot avoid grief. One cannot lead without experiencing it firsthand.

The key is how to do so with integrity—for the sake of both personal growth as well as organizational health.

WHY THE BIBLICAL PROPHETS?

So, why the biblical prophets? In all honesty, I can't say that I've really enjoyed reading the prophetic books of the Hebrew Scriptures over the years. The messages of "doom and gloom" were often hard to read, as well as challenging to understand from my twentieth and twenty-first century worldview. In seminary, I read them because I had to. Delving into their historical contexts certainly helped, but I'm a relational, empathic guy who didn't always want to swim in those turbulent waters. In early ministry, I read them devotionally because—well, they were part of God's word and I had to figure out why. After my heart attack, however, I read them intentionally because I was searching for answers.

Can you relate?

Pulling back from the details a bit, I discovered some impactful nuances within those prophetic books that fit more of my personality. The prophets in our Bible—both the Hebrew Scriptures as well as the New Testament—began to impress me in how they received their call from God, usually to do amazingly difficult and, at times, life-threatening tasks, and then, whether willingly or reluctantly, carried out their responsibilities despite tremendous sacrifices and significant personal losses, all to honor the greater divine mission. Prophets rocked the status quo. And they did so painstakingly.

Think about it. What would the Hebrew Scriptures look like if we removed the prophets from the story? They are the passionate voices of conviction and accountability announcing the consequences of judgment to a rebellious and recalcitrant people. They are the envoys of the compassionate invitations of God calling God's people to repent and return to their "first love." They are the negotiators of the divine mission, interpreting the behaviors of God's people through the lens of a larger metanarrative, which they themselves only glimpsed in snippets.

Some of the early prophets were classified as "judges" over Israel or Judah or both. Deborah, for example, wore both hats, as did Eli. Some of the prophets fulfilled their roles over decades, spanning the reigns of multiple kings and various empires. They needed to lead God's people through

INTRODUCTION

some of the darkest seasons of history . . . and they needed to do so often from the position of "second chair," or "third," or even "no chair," leading from the sidelines. For most of them—or rather, all of them, if you take into consideration the corporate experiences of the entire congregation of Israel—grief was their middle name. They had to navigate through the losses that came as a by-product of the changes their prophetic messages inspired (or didn't inspire, as was the case many times for rebellious Israel). How did they cope with their own grief sufficiently enough to lead a people through their corporate losses?

Take Jeremiah, for example. I could probably exert some smart-alecky witticism about how Jeremiah "wrote the book on Lamentation," but fundamentally, there's a much more definitive reason—namely, that this "weeping prophet" had served in his calling through some of the most difficult seasons in Israel's history leading up to and including exile. Major loss. How he interacted with God, and how he interacted with his own personal and "professional" grief because of his "job," with his often-unruly circumstances, with the charged recipients of his prophetic messages from God, and with the invasive influences of foreign kings and "gods," have much to teach us about healthy leadership in the face of change, growth, and loss.

There's also Anna, who gets married probably at the age of thirteen, as was typical, but whose husband dies seven years later. She spends the next eighty-four years as a widow practically living at the temple in Jerusalem, praying, and fasting and waiting for the Messiah to come and redeem Israel, bringing hope and restoration to all humanity. Then she meets Jesus.

And Samuel—who is born within the heartbreak of a barren mother, Hannah, who then gives him up in fulfillment of a promise she made to God within the bargaining phase of her grief—grows up serving in the temple before he even knew the Lord (1 Sam 2:18, 3:7). Sounds like many a preacher's kid, right? Yet, God calls him into the role of prophet and rears him into a major religious and political leader—a leader that wields such powerful influence over the politics of the day that with one message from God, he deposes King Saul and enthrones King David. Yet, his start came from within the grief of his mother—whose life within both barrenness and pregnancy embodied God's prophetic message before Samuel was even born.

There was also Huldah, a rather unique and fascinating prophetess in the Hebrew Scriptures and a contemporary of Jeremiah. It would be easy to read into the context of 2 Kgs 22 our twenty-first-century debates between complementarianism and egalitarianism, but the biblical fact remains that, according to the Jewish writers and editors, priests, prophets, and kings sought her out. Indeed, Huldah was a definitive power broker whose messages from the Lord evoked both judgment and seismic change in the land. And she's allotted a whole seven verses—twice—within the entire biblical narrative (2 Kgs 22:14–20; 2 Chr 34:22–28).

And how about Hosea? What was his call from God? "Go marry a prostitute and have children whose names will tell Israel how angry I am about their idolatrous and adulterous behaviors. Oh, and let them know that if they repent and return to me, I'm going to redefine what love can do" (my own paraphrase). Wow! Would we do that? Yet, by his obedience, Hosea taught an entire ethnic community—and an entire faith-based world for centuries to come—about the intentionality of God's covenantal, unconditional, abiding love.

Each of these prophets simultaneously had to be condemning of certain behaviors as they became a shepherd of God's judgment on the people of Israel (humanity), as well as encouraging to those same people as they sought to provide hope for a generation needing direction. What we learn by how they processed their roles, especially during those very difficult times, portrays both the character traits of leadership that would propel the entire congregation of Israel (and church) forward into its prophetic destiny, as well as the integrity of doing so within the humble constraints of being fully human and fully faithful in their response to the isolating factors that their messages and roles would inspire.

THIS BOOK

So, I write this book to explore those personal leadership qualities borne from both prophet and loss—with the goal of equipping those who lead with the ability to advance the divine mission within their context, and to do so with emotional integrity. I write first to pastors since the equipping of clergy and clergy-types is my personal mission as I live out my mandate to "mentor and multiply" for the sake of the movement of Jesus Christ's church. Yet, I am also passionate about leadership within the broader contexts of life, as well. So, I write secondly to leaders who are persons of faith within the corporate sectors—specifically, to those who have, or are willing to take on, the mantel of prophetic leadership in advancing the mission of their organization by remembering that organizations are made up of, and ultimately serve, the people who may be called to the same mission—both employees as well as clients and customers.

This book will explore how God uses our experiences of loss and grief to prepare us for deeper levels of leadership, equipping us to create environments within our churches and organizations that navigate change and growth in a healthier way. In fact, while each of the chapters is built around one of the five stages of grief (denial, anger, bargaining, depression, and acceptance) initially catalogued by Elisabeth Kübler-Ross in her groundbreaking work with death and dying,[4] the book is not a comprehensive view of the multiple facets of grief. Those types of books have already been written and are well worth reading. Rather, I'm looking at grief specifically through the lens of leadership—prophetic leadership in particular—and the ramifications personal loss has on a leader's ability to assist others through the impact of change within their organizations.

The book will also interplay with five of the biblical prophets that are critically a part of our faith story, eliciting wisdom from the "ancient paths" (Jer 6:16) that bring out the best in us as leaders. As a lead-in to each chapter, you'll be invited into my own fictionalized rendering of the biblical accounts of the call of these prophets, trying to extrapolate what might have been going on in their own thoughts and feelings as they engaged their respective prophetic ministries. These prophets were real people, fully human, and therefore subject to the full range of human emotions connected to grief and loss. My extrapolations seek to bring out their humanness, allowing God's prophetic messages to emerge from people who might have looked like us, felt like us, struggled like us, and grieved like us—rather than from unrelatable, iconic mystics whose words and paradigms intimidate us.

My goal is to make us all healthier, more authentic, leaders as together we embody God's prophetic message to a world—and a church—that seems to be forgetting who we are, why we're here, and to where God is leading us on mission.

In chapter 1, I focus on what I believe to be the most central theme of the entire biblical canon (and this book)—namely, that everything, absolutely everything, is about making disciples of Jesus Christ. Even grief and loss. I use the prophet Jeremiah as the biblical mentor, allowing his call to set the stage for the book. I also explore what it means to approach grief as a mosaic, rather than in linear or sequential terms.

---

4. See Kübler-Ross, *On Death and Dying*; and Kübler-Ross and Kessler, *On Grief and Grieving*.

In chapter 2, I take our discussion of grief as a mosaic into the core teaching of Jesus—that of forgiveness. I explore the redemptive nature of grief as well as how to live the lessons of loss by establishing an environment of accountable, redemptive grace. Forgiveness, for me, becomes the divine counter to the anger, resentment, and bitterness caused by loss. The New Testament prophetess Anna will be our mentor.

In chapter 3, I look at how we bargain with God and with our losses as we try to map out coping strategies to handle the emotions that are too difficult for us. Using the prophet Hannah as our guide, I explore what I call "congenital grief," the grief that some of us may be born into, or that our organizations are "born" into, and the assumptions that will help us lead in those transitions.

In chapter 4, I examine the grief stage of depression, both personally and organizationally, and how the prophet-leader's role is to walk *into* the darker seasons of life rather than to withdraw from them—and to do so with a set of tools that will connect us to the divine mosaic with faith. Huldah, the often missed contemporary of Jeremiah, will mentor us.

Finally, in chapter 5, I investigate the heart of Hosea as he negotiates with his personal life and the profound weight God's prophetic pronouncements of judgment will have on Israel. Doing so, I focus on the fundamental character trait of *hesed*—divinely inspired, covenantal love—and its implications for how leaders are to navigate through the tougher emotions of loss by embodying the mission to which they are called, leading us to acceptance of God's mosaic.

When a mission-minded leader compassionately understands and values the redemptive nature of their own pain, loss, and grief, they will be more equipped to guide their people through their grief toward the next phase of personal and corporate discipleship and growth. Ultimately, this is the work of spiritual formation and of missional leadership. And it's essential to the health and growth of any organization.

This is the purpose of *Prophet and Loss*.

A Prophet in Time: Jeremiah

THE ROOM VIBRATED WITHIN the close quarters of the makeshift sanctuary as the *minyan* recited the *Shema*—"Hear, O Israel, Adonai is our God, Adonai is one . . . " It was the centerpiece of their prayers this morning. They had gathered daily for years in the small annex built adjacent to Hilkiah's home. They would listen to a passage from the Torah—specifically, from a scroll of Shemot describing the deliverance of Adonai's people from bondage in Egypt, or a scroll of Bemidbar, the fourth book of Moses; both scrolls were gifts to Hilkiah that had been passed down from his grandfather, a legacy of his many years of high-level leadership within the temple and to remember who they were called to be. The sun's light would grow brighter soon, and the day's tasks would be before them. Then evening and morning would bring the cycle of life into its next chapter.

For now, though, Hilkiah, his brothers, his immediate circle of neighbors, and even his son, Jeremiah, followed the pattern of their fathers and grandfathers and great-grandfathers with precise rhythm and seasoned intonation. They were a family of priests, after all, proudly rooted in the house of Benjamin, even if, in the current times, they were somewhat challenged by the people's declining value for the traditions of their ancestors. Praying was a privilege. That's what Hilkiah had taught his son since the day he had taken his first steps. "You never know when Adonai is going to speak to his people again," he had said more than once over the years. "But we want to be ready when he does."

"Blessed are you, O Lord our God, Ruler of the universe . . . " Jeremiah watched his father's *tallit*-covered head bobbing as he canted the prayers with deep emotion and as the other men poured out their hearts for the redemption of Israel. So much was going on in the world that did not honor the Torah. So many—even of the congregation of their own village—were leaving the faith, leaving the call of Abraham to be a light to the nations, and pursuing the appetites of their eyes and the lusts of their hearts warned against by Moses in the holy words of the scroll of *Bemidbar*.[1] Their prayers lamented the loss of honor, even as they sensed that the Lord would indeed rise in judgment. Someday . . . perhaps soon.

Jeremiah, too, could feel the weight of those prayers—even as he smiled at his father's bouncing *tzitzit*, the tassels that reminded him of the commandments that had defined them as a people. Those commandments had called all the congregation of Israel to holiness, that they should never stray from the One who had called them by Adonai's name, that they should remain faithful to the One who was faithful to them. There was no option to Hilkiah, only obedience. Yet, he and his brothers felt increasingly alone in their desire to honor the Lord.

Jeremiah bowed his head, opened his hands before heaven, and then repeated what his father had modeled over the years. His own *tzitzit*, carefully and intentionally knotted on his *tallit* by his mother in preparation for his coming of age several years prior, began bouncing in rhythm to the group's chanting as he joined his father in weeping for the people of Israel. Yet, he wondered, would Israel indeed even hear anymore that "Adonai is our God?"

Anathoth was a rather small village when compared with other towns surrounding Jerusalem. Roughly three miles away from the Holy City, historically, it was one of the territories in the tribe of Benjamin given to the descendants of Aaron, and so was home to those who were known to be Levites, priests, caretakers of the temple. That Adonai would visit it with Adonai's prophetic message, however, surprised everyone, especially Jeremiah. But Adonai was not unaccustomed to surprising his people. Throughout the Torah were accounts of Adonai visiting the marginalized, calling the least expected. Abraham. Moses. Rachel. Hannah. Samuel. Ruth. Even David. Adonai chooses whomever Adonai so desires. Adonai favors whomever Adonai so chooses.

It began in his time of prayer—this nudging, this sense that Someone greater than he was speaking. Initially, the Voice was not audible, but deeply felt . . . and understood: *"Before I formed you in the womb I knew you, and before you were born, I consecrated you; I appointed you a prophet to the nations."*[2]

---

1. Num 15:39.
2. Jer 1:5.

The Voice was speaking not so much a greeting, but rather a revelation, a statement of fact based on an intentionality of purpose. The emphasis was not on Jeremiah, but on God; not on "you," but on "I": "Before *I* formed you . . . *I* knew you . . . *I* consecrated you . . . *I* appointed you . . . "

The declaration caused Jeremiah to shudder and to fall to the ground. His eyes squeezed shut and his arms wrapped around the back of his head as if protecting himself from whatever was coming at him. Yet, the word that was being spoken, while certainly overwhelming and awesome, was not violent. Rather, it was like an intense light that exposed every part of his being and yet embraced him with an even more intense assurance of peace. It was as if Holy Love itself was put to words and that Love was truth.

The Torah had told of times such as this. Abraham heard that Voice as it told him to pack up his things and his family and to travel to an unknown land . . . and again, when it told him to sacrifice his son, Isaac, the child of the promise. And Moses before a burning bush was captivated by a fire that did not consume. The Voice of the Lord spoke from that bush, and it called him by name into a mission that would change the trajectory of all of history.

Jeremiah wondered what that Voice wanted with *him*. A "prophet to the nations?" What did that mean? The thought unnerved him.

"Ah, Adonai Jehovah!" His voice was trembling, and his lips were developing a crust of sweat mixed with the dust from the floor of his room. "Truly I do not know how to speak, for I am only a boy."[3]

Jeremiah knew that similar reasoning had not worked well with Moses, but it was the first thing to come out of his mouth. Later, much later, he would remember those words with embarrassment, but for now his anxiety about the weight of responsibility such a mission would place on his shoulders made him question his readiness, even his worthiness. And it made him nauseous with fear. How could he be a prophet of the Most High? Who would listen to *him*? He was barely a young adult, far from being of the age to be classified with the elders of Israel. Who would give him, at his age, even the time of day? They would laugh at him. Or worse, they would become angry at his words and violent with their reactions.

"Do not say, 'I am only a boy'; for you shall go to all to whom I send you, and you shall speak whatever I command you. Do not be afraid of them, for I am with you to deliver you, says the Lord."[4]

---

3. Jer 1:6.

4. Jer 1:7–8.

It was as if the Voice had known his thoughts and named his fears. The call of Adonai was on him, like a mantel weighed down by the cries of the oppressed remnant of Adonai's people waiting to be delivered from an increasingly unrighteous and adulterous world. He felt that weight and its gravity pulled him deeper into prayer, deeper into a state of lamentation—a state that, unbeknownst to him at present, would last for decades to come.

In the solitude of that lamentation, Jeremiah sensed the presence of the Lord touching his mouth. It was a holy touch. It felt as if he was being kissed with the burning fire of an all-consuming love that would not rest until its foreshadowed ordination was complete. And with that kiss came the poetic announcement of his mission: *"Now I have put my words in your mouth. See, today I appoint you over nations and over kingdoms, to pluck up and to pull down, to destroy and to overthrow, to build and to plant."*[5]

Within that moment, Jeremiah's fate was sealed.

"Jeremiah."

"Yes, Adonai?" Jeremiah was still getting used to hearing the Voice.

"What do you see?"

Images began to dance around him, initially making him feel dizzy. Suddenly, and with great clarity, the image solidified before him.

"I see a branch of an almond tree."[6]

"You have seen well, for I am watching over my word to perform it."[7]

A second time the Voice came to Jeremiah, almost testing him—fine-tuning his new prophetic muscles. There would be other tests, for sure. Those tests would hone his ability to announce Adonai's message of judgment with the strength needed to be heard through the thick layers of mockery and denial. Those tests would refine his character. And they would scare the heck out of him. But for now . . .

"What do you see?"

"I see a boiling pot, tilted away from the north."[8] Jeremiah responded with more confidence, as the vision became clearer more quickly.

But that confidence would soon unravel.

"Out of the north disaster shall break out on all the inhabitants of the land. For now, I am calling all the tribes of the kingdoms of the north, says the Lord; and they shall come and all of them shall set their thrones at the

---

5. Jer 1:9–10.
6. Jer 1:11.
7. Jer 1:12.
8. Jer 1:13.

entrance of the gates of Jerusalem, against all its surrounding walls and against all the cities of Judah. And I will utter my judgments against them, for all their wickedness in forsaking me; they have made offerings to other gods and worshipped the works of their own hands."[9]

There it was. Judgment. The very thing that the *minyan* had been praying for, that his father and grandfather and great-grandfather had been praying for. It was coming. It was *here*.

And somehow Jeremiah was to be its ambassador. His stomach tied into knots once again. He began to hyperventilate, panicking from the ramifications of what was being laid out for him and for the people of Judah, his people. He, too, had prayed for this very thing. But for him to be the deliverer of the bad news? He imagined the grief, the intense pain of those facing the wrath of Adonai. Panic overwhelmed him and made him collapse. His heart was beating way too fast, even skipping out of the rhythm that he was accustomed to feeling, making him dizzy and lightheaded with fear. He wanted to vomit. No, he *had* to vomit.

After a moment, a wave of peace washed over him, settling him. The dizziness faded quickly. The nausea quelled. Still on his knees with his face close to the ground, he was aware of a presence near him. It calmed him. And then the Voice spoke again.

"Jeremiah, prepare yourself; stand up and tell them everything that I command you. Do not break down before them . . . or I will break you before them. And I for my part have made you today a fortified city, an iron pillar, and a bronze wall, against the whole land—against the kings of Judah, its princes, its priests, and the people of the land. They will fight against you; but they shall not prevail against you, for I am with you, says the Lord, to deliver you."[10]

Slowly getting to his feet, Jeremiah stood and tentatively made his way to the basin of water positioned on the corner table to the left of his bed, lit just enough to capture an opaque reflection of his face as he began to splash water on his eyes. A fortified city? An iron pillar? A bronze wall? Adonai clearly was seeing something in him that he could not see in himself. It seemed as if Adonai was asking him to be another Moses, or another Samson, or another Samuel. With puffy, bloodshot eyes, all Jeremiah could see was a *weeping* prophet.

---

9. Jer 1:14–16.
10. Jer 1:17–19.

Yet perhaps Adonai needed someone who would cry over the sins of his people, someone who would care deeply enough to stand in the gap of the broken relationship between humanity and Adonai and passionately plead with Adonai's people to return to their first love.

Apparently, that was to be him.

1

Denial

Everything is about making disciples for Jesus Christ. Everything.

But if you will not listen, my soul will weep in secret for your pride; my eyes will weep bitterly and run down with tears, because the Lord's flock has been taken captive.

—Jeremiah 13:17

In my prior book, *Mission Rift: Leading through Church Conflict*, I shared that "in my professional opinion, grief is the most central emotional, psychological, spiritual, cultural, and social-environmental milieu defining the human experience in the United States in the early twenty-first century.... Unresolved, post-traumatic, all-consuming hurt, pain, fear, brokenness, violations, and loss have colored our views of everyone and everything else, thereby preventing us from seeing beyond our own plight. We therefore act out, react to, and lash out against our interpretation of another's experience."[1]

From my experience of over thirty-five years in pastoral and consultative ministry, I believe that grief is, indeed, the single most important emotional process affecting our culture today. Grief is also the single most important leadership principle that leaders must learn as they navigate their organizations through change and growth. Leaders lead. They bring

1. Woolverton, *Mission Rift*, 62.

change into their organizations. Those changes always produce loss on some level. Good leaders evoke change and assist their organizations to process grief well. Bad leaders evoke change and neglect those emotional processes—and the people they are called to lead. While I always strive to be a good leader, in all transparency, I have been both.

Certainly, there are other emotions related to change. Many of them. But loss and a call to leadership seem intimately intertwined. And necessarily so. You cannot lead people through change without helping them grieve what they are leaving behind. And you cannot help others navigate grief if you haven't gone through it yourself. On an emotional level, you cannot take people where you yourself have not been.

The challenge, however, is that many leaders have a propensity to do two things—things that, ironically, give them the impression of success, but often betray the integrity of such success when done poorly: one, they keep a singular focus on achieving their goals and arriving at their mission (not a bad thing, right?); and yet two, they don't always have—or don't want to take—the time, or the patience, for the necessary "ending" emotions of grief related to moving themselves, or their people, forward.

And I get it. Grief is hard. It's deeply personal. It makes us vulnerable. Again, from *Mission Rift*:

> Grief also may come from within the pastor [or leader]. As leaders, many times our losses go unresolved, or they are sidelined in order to help others cope with their crises. Sometimes situations that we as leaders are called upon to mediate touch internal "nerves" that we become aware of only when those situations "push our buttons," causing a reaction.[2] Some losses are so embedded into our own past that they have affected our character development—revealing themselves through boundary crossing.[3] Grief can cause us to forget who we are, why we're here, and where we're going.[4]

Quite often, grief takes hostages. And the ransom to set them free is often very costly.

---

2. See Gauger, "Understanding the Internal, External," 24–50.
3. Gauger, "Understanding the Internal, External," 57–65.
4. Woolverton, *Mission Rift*, 62–63.

THE IMPACT OF DEATH

As I stated in the introduction, grief is one of the primary emotions of change. The more significant the change is, the more intense the grief response will be. They are the two interlocking human forces that dance the tango on the Marley of our family systems. We are most familiar with grief as it is related to death, yet grief comes at other times and in other contexts—both personal as well as professional. Death, of course, quite often expedites our grief lessons, so I use a lot of those images and stories in this book. So do the prophets in theirs. Yet, I will also share stories from other contexts as well—for they have a way of undermining our egos even more ferociously than death. Any context that involves change involves grief—whether we acknowledge it or not.

Let me say from the start, though: the topic of this book, and its content, may feel heavy for you. Of all topics, grief certainly is weighted. As you're reading the stories, which I encourage you to do, they may cause your own emotions of grief to surface. They may trigger your own memories of loss. Let me suggest that you jot down those emotions and memories. Allow them to hover with you over the lessons of this book. They are there for a reason—and they may help illustrate this book for you in more personal ways. Also, while the book is loaded with such heavier emotions, it's also filled with invitations for personal healing, as well as good ideas for sermons or for coaching or discipling your team members. If you prefer, read the book with a few friends, or a team of elders, or a book study group. This way you can speak into each other's journey.

Grief certainly comes to leaders in times of the death of loved ones. We are first and foremost human. We live in a human world. We live within human constraints. In fact, we negotiate with our own mortality—and the mortality of those we care about—all the time. When the stark, raw realities of death sneak into our lives, we must face the harsh truth that there are things that we just cannot fix—both personal and professional. And thus, my journey begins.

Bryan

Back in 1985, Bryan turned heads with his dirty blond mullet, mischievous grin, and shy, yet perfectly timed, dry wit. People genuinely loved him. And he loved life. Especially sports. He was completely a teenager, for sure, with the rush of hormones and a penchant for heavy metal music. Yet, he had an innocent faith that was open to what God had in mind for each day. He and his brother Eric immediately found their way into my heart. I was their youth pastor and yet I quickly was drawn into their lives much more as an "older" brother. I was twenty-three at the time and I had connected with their church as part of my field education while in seminary. Youth group and youth retreats became energized when Eric and Bryan attended, and they had the unique ability to draw others into the group with them. I absolutely loved those guys.

After I had graduated from seminary and moved into full time ministry, our paths separated, though we remained in contact—just not with the regularity of what Facebook, Instagram, and email provide today. In time, Eric and Bryan graduated from high school and moved into the next phases of their lives—college and work.

Then came Wednesday night, November 10, 1993. Bryan and his good friend, Seann, were working a side job at a local video store in their hometown. Sometime during that evening, one—or two (it's still not known)—individuals came in and stabbed both of those boys repeatedly, leaving them to die in the forced silence of their cold murders.

I still remember approaching Eric, his other brother, Andy, and their mom and dad in the visitation line just prior to Bryan's funeral. The deep feelings of sadness—mixed with a rage that I felt toward the perpetrator, a rage the intensity of which I had never felt before—were overwhelming to me. As Eric saw me, he threw his arms around me and together we cried tears of unrelenting pain—an experience that replicated itself successively with each family member. These were the emotions that I continued to experience for weeks, and then months, as Bryan's photo was broadcast on the evening news, and as the media discussed the progress of the investigation.

To date, these cases are still unsolved. And both families—and all who knew Bryan and Seann, including me—remain unsettled by the lack of closure to these ever-present open wounds.

Alex[5]

When I first met Alex in 1988, he already had a full-fledged twentieth-century teenage edgy attitude. His adolescent pseudo-sarcasm was a cover-up,

---

5. Most of these names throughout this section are changed out of respect for their families. For the ones that were not changed, I have received permission to reference

DENIAL

I believe, for a heart that was searching, but suspicious. I saw the searching through his consistent faithfulness in attending just about every youth group meeting, retreat, ski trip, and movie outing. It took me four solid years as his pastor to see a tangible sign that I was being let into his circle of trust.

That sign came after a very challenging mission trip to Puerto Rico. While there were experiences on that trip that, for those of us leading it, were quite traumatic at times (for example, major infestations of mosquitoes, roaches the size of dill pickles, clusters of geckos climbing the walls of our dorm, three trips to different remote emergency rooms due to injuries, and a visit from the local police at two in the morning searching the neighborhood for the family member of a deceased individual), it was a significant turning point for Alex. About two months after we returned, he came to my house to tell me that he wanted to study international relations in college. Diplomacy. Apparently, the trip I was still recovering from somehow had inspired a call in Alex.

The following year Alex had the opportunity to travel to Russia for one of his classes. It was such a joy for me to help him financially be able to go. As a response to my support, when he returned from the trip, he came to my home again to share with me all about his experiences. I had never, ever, heard him talk so incessantly, with excitement and passion . . . and laughter. That moment brought great joy to my heart. Then he reached into his bag, pulled out a copy of the Bible translated into the Russian language, and gave it to me as a gift. "I saw this and knew I wanted to get it for you," he said. I was so, so touched that I was speechless. After a moment and with a smile on my face, I replied, "Alex, countless people have given their lives to bring Bibles *into* Russia. What are you doing bringing them back *out*?" We laughed together. And I realized yet again how God transforms lives right in front of my eyes through an investment of love and grace.

Then came March 1995. On his way back to school from a spring break, the driver of the car in which he was a passenger lost control of the vehicle. The car rolled over several times, throwing Alex from the car. He died that evening from traumatic brain injuries. And part of my heart died with him.

Casey

One of Alex's best friends was Casey. Casey, Alex, and one of their other friends, John, were the "Three Musketeers." They drove me up a wall with their stories.

their antics, their practical jokes, and their edgy attitudes. And I loved each one of them. From my first encounter with Casey, I learned that he was a profound negotiator. Clearly, he was destined for some career in sales. He could talk around just about any objection and justify just about any behavior with smooth, articulate skills.

Professionally, Casey did indeed go on into sales—and often, I would be one of his early targets. "Dave, you really need to consider camping. I have a great opportunity for you . . ." What I loved about those calls was not so much the products that Casey was trying to sell me, but what inevitably would happen after his sales pitch. We talked about life. It was during one of the conversations that he and I had after Alex's death that drew me even deeper into Casey's journey. He talked about his faith in God and the sense that God wanted something more for him. It was then that I suggested that maybe God was calling him into a form of ministry. "Sales and ministry," I had joked with him, "they share some of the same skills, you know." Casey actually allowed me to explore the possibilities with him. He even let me pray with him.

We continued those conversations for quite some time until mid-August 2000. I remember receiving *that* phone call—very vividly. I was at home putting up a chair rail in my bedroom when my phone rang. It was Casey's father calling to tell me that Casey was in the ICU at the hospital. He had suffered a significant brain aneurysm and was currently unconscious. They did not expect him to survive.

My wife, Kristine, and I immediately drove to the hospital where we prayed—and cried—at his bedside. Casey passed away not long after.

Standing at the pulpit at Casey's funeral service, after sharing a message that was profoundly difficult for me, I sobbed uncontrollably during the singing of the closing song. The weight of having lost Bryan, then Alex, and now Casey was overpowering for me.

THE WEIGHT OF LOSS ON MY LEADERSHIP

The deaths of Bryan, Alex, and Casey had three things in common. First, each of them died very prematurely. Second, even though they were beyond their teenage years when they died, they were most definitely still my "youth group kids," and I deeply cared for them. Third, even though during my clinical training as an emergency room and trauma chaplain I had been with multiple families facing traumatic scenarios equal or worse than those faced by Bryan, Alex, and Casey, the deaths of these three guys had rocked my faith to the core, forcing me to reevaluate not only my theology of loss, but whether or not I wanted to open my heart again to the people I was called to serve.

In all honesty, I was angry—angry at God, in particular, primarily because I didn't know to whom else I could direct my pain. Initially, my anger was self-righteous: "I had poured energy and countless time into these guys. Lord, why did you take them?!" Gradually, I realized that my anger was a cover-up for fear. Specifically, I was afraid of the intimacy of death—that death and grief would get so close to me that I would feel its talons closing in on those that I care deeply about, and that I could do nothing about it. It wasn't just my own mortality that I was being forced to face, but rather the mortality of those within the inner circles of my heart.

While I processed my intense emotions, I had to continue working. I was a pastor, after all, and life and ministry moved on. And, of course, there were other funerals that would challenge my pastoral sparring with the cloaked specter of grief.

There was Kenny, a six-month-old child who died tragically from shaken baby syndrome at the hands of his babysitter. Walking with Kenny's family through their intense grief was heart wrenching. While charges and sentencing put the perpetrator into prison, nothing ever would provide justice for Kenny's parents nor compensate for such loss.

And there was Donald, a young husband and father of three who had hidden his depression so well that no one anticipated that one day he would come home from work, eat dinner with his family, get into his car, drive to the Route 30 bridge that crosses the Susquehanna River, and, leaving the car running, get out of the car and sprint to the edge of the bridge, jumping to his death.

And there was Kay, my colleague and friend. On her way home from leading a church growth workshop, she was killed in a traffic accident. Ironically, the other car was driven by members of the youth group of one of my dearest friends on their way home from a youth event. Sadly, no one was able to discern why she went through the stop light. Local police officers were charged with the duty of going to Kay's home to inform her husband—news that would devastate him, and so many of us who knew Kay, for years to come.

And there was Frank, a young leader that I had discipled to take over our leadership team at church, who developed brain cancer and died within the first year of his new role.

And after Frank, there was another young leader, Jason, who I had encouraged to take Frank's place in leadership. A few short months after assuming the role, Jason was diagnosed with a brain tumor and died soon after.

And after Jason, I had asked another leader to take over the leadership team, George, who, within just a few years, lost both of his children—one to an aneurysm, the other to an unexpected cancer diagnosis.

(I actually began to question whether or not to ask anyone else to fill that leadership position!)

And there was Nicole, a young wife and mother of two sweet girls, that I had discipled into another leadership position at the church, and who definitively redefined what next generation leadership looked like in that congregation. Nicole, however, died of an aggressive form of breast cancer. Preaching her funeral message on the very steps where just thirteen years prior I had officiated her and her husband's wedding evoked emotions within me too difficult to put into words.

These situations of death and their impact on me, however, were only part of the story. Early on in ministry, the congregation I served began to grow significantly—from three hundred in worship to around two thousand within the span of ten years. During that decade, my job description changed six times, as did my voice at the table of leadership—which diminished progressively. Infrastructure shifts, executive responses to those shifts, personality clashes, leadership style differences, staff exits, and new staff hires were becoming routine processes as we accommodated the incremental growth. With every shift, transitional grief became normative as we constantly renegotiated boundaries and adjusted to new rhythms.

By the time I started my next church assignment, I had realized that my personal identity during the prior fifteen years had been so intimately married to my ministry that the move to my new role felt seismic. Preaching three services to a large crowd was exciting and dynamic. Going from there to a church with a worship attendance of two hundred and forty, a church that was struggling with immobilizing conflict, felt like a culture shock. It took quite a bit of prayer and spiritual direction to reorient myself around my call, rather than the context and perceptions of my call, as the driving force behind my identity. I had to let go of what had become a false image of myself, a two-dimensional icon of my identity that lacked the personal depth that only God could give me.

A lot had to die during that season of my life. Loss, in fact, became an iconoclast—a constant force that God used to shed the cherished idols that I thought were important, to create space for what God thought was important, and for a mission that would require total surrender of my heart and life to that cause.

THE GIFT OF GRIEF

The challenge for me was that I was—and still am—a relational leader. My leadership style has me building relationships, and in many respects, learning to love genuinely the people that I am called to serve. By personality, I'm an introvert (though I live within an extroverted role). By training, I'm an equipper. By spiritual gifts, I'm a leader, a teacher, a prophet, and an evangelist. By temperament, I'm an empathic healer. The relational skills that I have are grand strengths that have served me well as a pastor, a leader, an educator, and most especially, as a church conflict consultant. I'm highly intuitive and easily improvisational. I can quickly assess an organization, a room, a couple, or a person, tuning in empathically to what is the source of their struggles and, through the art of questioning, move participants toward pathways of healing and restoration. I've learned to differentiate and clarify boundaries to equip healthier responses and systems to facilitate overall growth of the person or the organization.

The problem was that my greatest strength was also my most challenging weakness. Grief made my empathy numb when it got too personal.

Most certainly, I saw it with the deaths of people I cared about. Yet, I also discovered it when I would lead the congregations I served through significant changes and inevitably would take personally the reactions of those who were challenged by those changes.

It was when I began to face intentionally into my own grief work that the Lord seemed to guide me into a new way of looking at loss and leadership. The catalysts for that deeper appreciation for grief ironically came when I reflected on two more deaths.

Prophet and Loss

Kelly

Kelly was the eight-year-old daughter of two of my dearest friends, Rob and Lisa. Kelly bravely faced into brain cancer until it ultimately took her life in September 1993. So many prayers had been lifted up for Kelly, yet healing did not come in the way we all had hoped. Prior to her passing, however, Kelly had a dream that she was eating at a table for two with Jesus in heaven. That dream was a redemptive gift amid heartache and unfathomable pain. It was the process of walking through the impact of Kelly's death with her mom and dad, being invited into the depths of their pain and the vulnerability of their loss,[6] that I began to ask different questions—of God, of myself, of grief itself.

Through these exchanges, I had come to realize that grief is actually God's gift for helping us through the transitions that are so much a part of our human experience. Grief is a healing tool given to us in the moments when we need it most, especially when life does not make sense and we have no patience even to pursue such deeper understanding. Grief is a gift of grace, a moniker of favor in a time when we don't feel favored.

Betty

At the other spectrum of life was Betty, who, in her seventies, died from metastatic breast cancer a week after Kelly. Being present with her at the moment of her passing enabled me to see—literally see—a faithful follower of Jesus being welcomed home into the embrace of her Lord.

I had been asked to come to the house when Betty's husband, Jon, had been told by the hospice nurse that Betty was "actively dying." I arrived around seven-thirty that evening. They had set up a hospital bed in the living room and Jon was sitting by the head of the bed, gently caressing his wife's arm. Their three adult children were camped out in various parts of the living and dining rooms, keeping vigil. I had been in this exact scenario so many times over the years both in my clinical work as well as during my pastoring, so I pretty much knew what to expect. A chair was set up at the foot of the bed, so I sat and began to read Scriptures and say prayers and to offer comfort during this emotionally difficult time, creating a space for whatever they needed that time to be.

---

6. For the full story, see Bair, *Table for Two* and *Grief is a Dancer*.

Betty was fully medicated, her eyes partly open, yet glazed over with the vacancy offered by progressive dosing of morphine. Her breathing was labored. The night went on mostly in quiet conversations spotted throughout hours of silence. A few minutes before two o'clock in the morning, Betty's breathing suddenly changed. It was time. I knew it. So, I gently spoke into the silence, "It's time. Her breathing has changed. It won't be long now."

Jon immediately leaned in toward Betty. "What do I do?" he asked, his eyes looking at me helplessly, filling with tears.

"Talk to her, Jon. Tell her you love her. Tell her it's okay to go, that you'll be okay. I'm sure she can hear you."

Jon and his kids tentatively did just that, unsure of what to expect—wanting to be there, and yet scared by the moment. I remained seated at the foot of the bed, giving them their space for this private expression of love, mixed with fear.

Just as the room's grandfather clock chimed two o'clock, something occurred that I will never forget. I saw a beam of light coming from over my right shoulder behind me and shining onto the bed. Immediately, I felt a breeze of cool air rushing past me, and I started to shake uncontrollably, as if I had chills from a fever. It was not from fear, for I had been in this situation so many times; but I could not stop that deep quaking in my body. It felt like I was in the presence of something very holy. In fact, I felt almost paralyzed, unable to move.

Betty's eyes suddenly opened fully, and she stared at the source of that light. Previously glazed over, her eyes were now quite clear, and they looked past me with a sense of recognition and joy. She pulled herself up as if wanting to sit up and her mouth opened as if she was trying to say something. Jon and the others seemed unaware of what was going on. Caught up in their grief, their heads were down and they were weeping. The experience lasted only about a minute, though it seemed much longer, and then Betty laid back down, closed her mouth and her eyes, and she was gone. Just then, the beam of light disappeared, the breeze stopped, and my shaking ended as suddenly as it had started.

While I have been with dozens and dozens of people at the moment of their passing, this was the single event that redefined death for me, and reminded me that in spite of our human limitations, we are part of a story that is much bigger than us.

And that story must frame our leadership within the organizations that we serve, as well as who we are as the prophetic leaders God calls us to be within the divine mission. Grief actually is God's gift of God's own presence, given progressively and redemptively to guide us through our journey from brokenness to wholeness, from fracture to forgiveness, from abandonment to an embrace of grace. As such, I would argue that *grief is a spiritual discipline* that's designed to draw us closer to God, closer to the One who defines us, closer to the Only One who can redeem our loss and frame our pain within a grander mosaic. In Hebrew terms, grief facilitates shalom.

Yet, as leaders, we are not quick in receiving such a gift. Nor do we tend to want to engage this particular spiritual discipline.

THE FOUR PRIMARY WAYS WE AVOID GRIEF

Facing into grief—personally as well as professionally—takes a leader to a whole new level of leadership. In all honesty, for many years I tried to avoid grief. I *had* to deal with grief-related situations, of course. Funerals, hospice visits, traumas, and being with people during their dying processes all were a natural part of my work as a pastor.

And so were the grief processes that were necessarily a part of every transition that I was called upon to lead in the churches where I served—most especially during the seasons of conflict that were so much a part of the congregations that I was either serving, or with which I was consulting.

As a leader, I led change. That made me a *causal agent* for grief—both for the congregation as well as for myself. For example, in one of my congregations, there was a "prayer rail" that spanned the full length of the front of the sanctuary, dividing the platform (chancel) from the pews (nave). Doing weddings, baptisms, funerals, and children's programs were exceptionally challenging. As the congregation grew and ministries required expanded space, I led a process that ultimately took out that rail, opening up the space for those ministries. This decision brought up some intensely negative reactions from several of the congregation members—reactions that were aimed at me.

Specifically, my "change leadership" evoked multiple grief emotions, many of which I, personally, did not like, nor did I deal with well (although professionally, I was good at presenting myself as a non-anxious presence during those changes).

What I've learned is that leaders tend to avoid grief in four primary ways:

1. We deny it.
2. We sublimate it.
3. We displace it.
4. We self-medicate it.

It's important to look at each of these avoidant defense mechanisms briefly as we face into our grief work so as to name our coping strategies and make the necessary choices related to their effectiveness. Doing so will increase our overall personal leadership capacity as well as equip us to facilitate change more effectively within our organizational contexts.

Avoidant Behavior #1: We Deny It

Denying, or ignoring, grief is one of the most common defense mechanisms employed by leaders—especially those who define themselves as "apostolic" in their ministry calling,[7] or score a high D (dominance) in their DiSC profile.[8] Many strong visionary leaders convince themselves that they don't have time for the emotions that threaten to derail the achieving of their goals. Some believe that, while grief certainly can be substantiated and real, it's not something that they believe "deserves" the time or reflection so many others feel is important.

In leaders, denial can reveal itself in multiple ways. One form of denial may involve repression—where leaders may push harder emotions like grief deeper into their unconscious. They may deny the impacts of grief on their own emotional wellbeing, while pushing their pain into the recesses of their mind and heart, convincing themselves that they're fine, or that they'll deal with their losses later.

Similarly, leaders may try to rationalize grief—choosing to intellectualize it, objectifying the feeling, rather than genuinely owning the emotion. A person might say, "How am I feeling? Well, as expected, I'm going through the stage of denial, not really accepting the reality of how my life has been changed, but I'm anticipating that I'll get over this soon as I find a new job" . . . rather than, "How am I feeling? I'm devastated by this! I did not anticipate getting fired! I don't understand what I did wrong. It's confusing the heck out of me!"

---

7. For example, see Knopf, "Learn about the Fivefold Ministry."
8. For example, see "DiSC Styles."

Leaders may also trivialize losses—minimizing, or making fun of, their (or other's) grief or pain. Minimizing emotions, whether our own or someone else's, typically is a sign that our anxiety is running high and we're struggling to convince ourselves that we're better than we are. Sometimes minimizing is rooted in our family of nurture, where most of us have learned how to deal with loss. "Don't be a baby!" or "Walk it off!" or "Man up!" become the mantras that define how we think we're supposed to respond to pain. Yet, those mantras force us into cognitive dissonance with the genuine feelings of loss that are competing for acknowledgement.

Each of these expressions, it's important to understand, is a coping strategy—as we overplay a hand that cannot be dealt with more directly.

Regardless of which form of this defense mechanism is employed, denial is quite common. In fact, it's one of the first layers of the grief process as originally discerned by Elisabeth Kübler-Ross in her classic studies on trauma, death, and dying.[9] In short, it's normal, even when it doesn't always appear so. And it is the root of all the other three common avoidant strategies.

From a leadership perspective, denial is our mind's (and heart's) way of protecting itself—at least until it has a chance to define the parameters of grief and loss in ways that make sense to us, or are less confusing, or, more specifically, will cause us less anxiety. It doesn't ignore the reality of the loss, necessarily; rather, it compartmentalizes it until the internal emotional chaos begins to stabilize. It is vitally important that we respect denial—for it's a God-designed tool to help us face what we need to face in the timing of when we are able to face it.

In my experience, anxiety really is at the root of most defense mechanisms. Think about it. Even the term *defense* mechanism assumes that we are needing to protect ourselves from a force that we cannot control.

And leaders tend to want to be in control—at least in terms of their own emotions and circumstances.

Avoidant Behavior #2: We Sublimate It

In psychological terms, sublimation is a defense mechanism that "involves channeling unwanted or unacceptable urges into an admissible or

---

9. See Kübler-Ross, *On Death and Dying*, and Kübler-Ross and Kessler, *On Grief and Grieving*.

productive outlet."[10] It's the coping strategy of substitution and tends to be a more acceptable form of denial.

In leaders, for example, the difficult emotional processes of grief may get channeled into over-functioning, taking on additional projects, or working longer hours. Workaholism in leadership circles is often touted as a value, deeming it a more acceptable outlet for unprocessed grief. What organization—including the church—doesn't like to see their leaders being highly productive? In fact, society itself subtly promotes sublimation. Typically, businesses only provide up to three days off for bereavement and then expect employees to return to the productivity of work. Not every leader who overworks is sublimating, necessarily; but working beyond the normal rhythms of their typical routine could be a symptom of avoidance.

In extreme forms, leaders will try to convince others (and themselves) that they are genuinely fine with their loss and end up behaving in ways that are the opposite of what they feel. Their reaction formation can become a set up for denial as they try to "fake it until they make it."

Sublimation is a temporary fix, no matter how long it lasts. Ultimately, the internal disconnection from how we genuinely feel pushes against our coping façade. This could lead either to an honest moment of integration, or perhaps episodes of decompensation leading to an emotional breakdown, if not processed well.

Avoidant Behavior #3: We Displace It

Unresolved, unprocessed grief is like a boiling pot that has a lid on it. When the pressure inside the pot gets too overwhelming, steam pushes its way out through the sides of the lid. Lifting the lid might bring about an initial burst of hot steam, which may burn or threaten to burn for a moment, but then the pressure in the pot normalizes to its environment. By not lifting the lid, the pressure seeks to normalize itself in whatever way it can—usually by pushing the steam out into multiple directions. By doing so, the pressure gets *displaced*.

Leaders tend to be high controllers. When faced with situations, or emotions, that they cannot control, the internal cognitive dissonance can cause a pressure that may force itself out in ways that affect others—causing peripheral damage. Typically, this pressure build-up expresses itself in anger outbursts that are misdirected either at other people (or even God),

---

10. "Sublimation."

or at less significant events that trigger the expression of the grief emotions meant for something or someone else. In other words, we find other people or events to be the receivers of our venting of emotions that belong somewhere else.

Often, leaders select others who are below their power grid, giving them an opportunity to feel in control when, in fact, internally they feel out of control. For example, a person's spouse at home may yell at them about some issue while they remain silent in the moment, only to go to work and then yell at the secretary for not filing a paper where it needed to go. Or they may select people that they are closest to since, deep down, they have an internal security that that person will not abandon them during a time when they feel vulnerable and anxious.

Avoidant Behavior #4: We Self-Medicate It

Another avoidant behavior common to leaders involves how we self-medicate to cope with the emotions that we are unable or unwilling to face directly. Prescription pain killers and tranquilizers form a growing class of abused pharmaceuticals, yet they are not alone in the category of self-medication. Illicit drugs, pot, alcohol, porn, indiscriminate sex, cutting, and other practices are used to numb emotional pain while hiding from the real sources that cause such pain.

Self-medication is a cover-up coping strategy. We use it when we want to cover up our pain, when we feel out of control of our situations (or life, in general), and when we want to escape the harsh realities that make us feel vulnerable. Then, these behaviors often can develop into addictions that add layers to our patterns of denial, making us feel further trapped into an unproductive loop.

Similarly, leaders may act out with behaviors that intentionally push the limits on risk and danger. They start to pursue experiences that cause a rush of adrenalin to compensate for how they may feel out of control in other areas of their lives. Such acting out behaviors may scale from the more socially acceptable—like taking up skydiving or cliff diving, to the other extreme—like engaging in risky sexual behaviors, shoplifting (in the initial phases), or embezzlement. Reactivity of this nature challenges the emotions of grief—forcing an internal "duel" with the emotions that we are unwilling to accept. When such behaviors are a change in the leader's "normal" hobbies or routines, they become "red flags" to those who are close to them, signaling that the leader needs interventional support.

Again, all of these are coping strategies and are used to avoid the painful emotions related to loss. Importantly, any of these avoidant behaviors may end up sabotaging our leadership, ministry, marriage, or life—whether intentionally or inadvertently.

I must admit that I have employed many of these strategies to some degree at various times over the years. How about you?

So, how do we reorient ourselves to face into both our calling to lead as well as the harsher emotions that come with that calling? The prophet Jeremiah may mentor us.

A PROPHET IN TIME

The prophet Jeremiah had the difficult task of sharing confrontational messages of judgment and devastation to a people who, by and large, did not want to hear what he had to say. For over forty years, from around 626 BCE through the fall of Jerusalem and the destruction of the temple in 586 BCE, and through the span of five kings—Josiah, Jehoahaz, Jehoiakim, Jehoiachin, and Zedekiah—he desperately tried to call God's people back into alignment with God's heart, with God's mission for the people of Israel and Judah, and with genuine worship of the Most High God.

Prior to Jeremiah's ministry, the people of Judah had front-row seats to the dismantling of the Northern Kingdom of Israel by the Assyrian Empire. Yet, they really didn't learn. The people's chronic resistance, their stubborn sinful rebellion, and their insistence in the worship of idols and foreign gods, however, eventually would bring about such severe judgment that now Judah too would be conquered by a foreign nation (Babylon), exiled from their long-forsaken "promised land," and excommunicated from the house of God that had once welcomed their sacrifices and prayers.

God's prophetic call on Jeremiah was to deliver the messages of both the consequences of Judah's behavior, as well as an invitation to repent and return: he was "to pluck up and to pull down, to destroy and to overthrow," yet also "to build and to plant" (Jer 1:10). Yet, most of his hearers were not in support of his message. Even the people from Anathoth, his hometown, demanded that he shut down his ministry and silence his demoralizing words of judgment: "You shall not prophesy in the name of the Lord, or you will die by our hand" (Jer 11:21). Religious leaders, other prophets, and generally, all the other people who heard his message "laid hold of him, saying 'You must die!'" (Jer 26:8), and they tried to get the temple officials to sentence him to death (Jer 26:11). Yet amid that, Jeremiah issued another invitation to "amend your ways and your doings, and obey the voice of the Lord your God, and the Lord will change his mind about the disaster that he has pronounced against you" (Jer 26:13).

Through it all, the Voice he listened to despite all the resistance, was that of the One who had called him, gifted him, and promised to be with him: "Jeremiah, prepare yourself; stand up and tell them everything that I command you.... And I for my part have made you today a fortified city, an iron pillar, and a bronze wall, against the whole land—against the kings of Judah, its princes, its priests, and the people of the land. They will fight against you; but they shall not prevail against you, for I am with you, says the Lord, to deliver you" (Jer 1:17-19). This Voice enabled him, in one of his most dire situations, to simply respond: "But as for me, here I am in your hands. Do with me as seems good and right to you.... For in truth the Lord sent me to you to speak all these words in your ears" (Jer 26:14-15).

As a leader, what voice are *you* listening to?

The role of the prophet may not necessarily be glamorous like that of an apostle, or embracing like that of a shepherd, or knowledgeable like that of a teacher, or winsome like that of an evangelist. Yet, the prophet plays a significant function within the systems of the congregation or organization.[11]

The prophet wears a mantel—and bears a message—that burdens their soul. Deeply. Prophets are not fortune tellers. Their job is not to predict the future, but rather to feel the weight of the present in light of the divine mission. The divine mission is the movement that propels God's people forward—toward the destiny that God has ordained. It is the combination of the Great Commission (Matt 28:16-20) and the Great Commandment (Matt 22:36-40, and later redefined in John 13:34-35), and it forms the central job description for the church—regardless of the believer's context. Wherever a follower of Jesus is, *there* is the divine mission field.

Prophets, by God's design, hold the people accountable not only *for* that mission, but *to* that mission. Therefore, ironically, genuine prophets are more concerned about the *present* than the future, more concerned with getting God's people to align themselves with God's purposes, with God's

---

11. For an amazing perspective on what they call "trioptic leadership," see Blair et al., "Prophets, Priests, and Kings," 127-45.

plans, with God's heart *now*. Any future "prediction" actually is a prophetic envisioning of what will play out if God's people continue to align themselves away from God's purposes, plans, and heart.

In our culture today, I believe that leadership comes necessarily with the mantel of prophet. Leaders must care more about the weight of the present situation of their organization—the alignment of its mission, its vision, and its team with the values consistent with God's greater cause—than about themselves, than about the profitable gains, than about *anything* else. Present alignment to that divine mission *today* is what will enable the organization to bear greater fruit *tomorrow*.

That's why leadership is best done within a team-based model. Not every individual leader has the capacity to do all the functions required to navigate their organizations forward on mission. Nor should they. To put all the responsibilities for the success or failure of an organization onto the shoulders of one individual is simply ludicrous. At the same time, it is also no longer wise to assume that organizations require a linear hierarchical leadership structure. Team-based models of leadership better facilitate the overall functioning and flow of organizational objectives—no matter the size of the organization. Having a prophetic perspective within that leadership base is essential.

Interpreting Jeremiah's experiences within our context today, therefore, we learn that being a prophet in any organization is about leading people through a *discipleship process* that helps them remember who they are in Christ, why the organization exists beyond the product it produces, and how the organization participates in the greater design of what God is doing in the world. By viewing Jeremiah's role over the span of decades, he gives us a platform for viewing our role longitudinally as well.

For followers of Jesus, developing a divine mission mind-set is critically important for organizational leadership. The local church, for example, was never intended to be the *end* of the process of discipleship, but rather a *means to an end*. The church is a movement of God's Spirit, a vehicle by which God accomplishes God's mission of multiplying disciples for the transformation of the world through divinely-empowered acts of *self-sacrificial love* invasively perpetrated by lives changed by Christ. Indeed, such multiplication is meant to be exponential, rather than incremental (Matt 25:14–30; Acts 9:31; 12:24; John 6:1–15)—empowered by the Holy Spirit.

EVERYTHING IS ABOUT MAKING DISCIPLES

Playing out that divine mission, therefore, in simple terms, is this foundational premise: we must begin to see that *everything, absolutely everything, is about making disciples for Jesus Christ. Everything.* Now, let me briefly demythologize what I mean by that statement.

According to Matthew's Gospel (28:18–20), just before his ascension, Jesus issued to his disciples what we now know as the Great Commission: "And Jesus came and said to them, 'All authority in heaven and on earth has been given to me. Go therefore and make disciples of all nations, baptizing them in the name of the Father and of the Son and of the Holy Spirit, and teaching them to obey everything that I have commanded you. And remember, I am with you always, to the end of the age.'" Jesus's challenge to his disciples was to go and replicate in others what they had seen him do in them. Within the rabbinic culture of that day the language of "disciples" made sense. Students apprenticed with a rabbi, learned the mantle of teaching connected to what that rabbi had learned from his rabbi, and then reproduced that model in the ensuing generations. It was actually a great model of linear reproduction, a type of rabbinic succession plan, if you will. The model worked well for the early church—and for the generations of Christians yet to come as the movement spanned the centuries into modern times.

In today's culture, "disciple-ship" needs to be reframed a bit. Personally, I reframe it using the language of *mentoring*. Same principle though—Jesus wants his followers to go into all the world (see the layering approach modeled in Acts 1:8) and reproduce in others what was taught to us (2 Tim 2:2). This ever-expanding movement multiplies God's renewing influence within the world thereby drawing more and more people into reflecting the heart of God within their daily lives and into partnership in carrying out God's grander mosaic.

Therefore, within our context of grief and loss, we cannot mentor the next generation of followers with what we ourselves have not learned. Mentoring requires that we ourselves have been mentored—and that we have learned the lessons sufficiently to have integrated them into our own journey of faith and life.

As such, four aspects of that discipleship-mentoring are important to hear:

1. *Only God can change a heart and life.* "Disciple-making" is always initiated by the Holy Spirit. The Spirit is the active agent producing heart-change in the life of a person. Our role is to mentor forward those within whom the Holy Spirit has already initiated life change. Since we don't always know in advance who those persons might be, we live out the initial phases of our mentoring through acts of invitation and connection—telling the stories of Jesus, sharing how Jesus has changed our lives, inviting people into ongoing, loving relationships with ourselves and others, and then watching for those who respond to the nudging of the Spirit within them. We then come alongside those persons and continue nurturing their faith journey to the point of them going out and doing the same thing with others. Such invitations and connections can start within any context of life—including (and perhaps, especially) within experiences or seasons of loss.

2. *God never wastes anything.* All our experiences—the good, the bad, and the ugly—are soil within which God germinates new growth. As I shared above, God is the only One who can change a person's heart. God is the only One who can lead a person into and through the processes of spiritual formation—and all spiritual formation processes involve the "leaving of the old" and moving on to "the new" that God is birthing (2 Cor 5:17). It's God's process, after all. So, we need to discover what God is doing and join in as God brings beauty and new life from brokenness and ashes (Isa 61:3).

3. *Discipleship is never meant to occur in a vacuum.* Whatever God nurtures in us is not just for us. It's meant to be given to others. This, I believe, is the essential "part two" of the "call" description of Eph 4:11–13. The callings the Holy Spirit bestows on the people of faith—apostles, prophets, evangelists, pastors, and teachers—are "to equip the saints for the work of ministry, *for building up the body of Christ*, until all of us come to the unity of the faith and of the knowledge of the Son of God, to maturity, to the measure of the full stature of Christ" (italics mine). That work of discipleship-mentoring has a context and that context is the church. Spiritual formation is a mutually shared process.

4. *The prophet is first an equipper.* In truth, we cannot hold anyone accountable for what we have not taught them. Before we prophets can pronounce judgment, we must hold ourselves accountable to the need

to equip the people in what it means to follow in the footsteps of Jesus, the "pioneer and perfecter of our faith" (Heb 12:2). We prophets must "consider him who endured such hostility against himself from sinners, so that [we] may not grow weary or lose heart" (Heb 12:3) when looking at the conditions of the church or world. Faith leaks over time when it is not nurtured. Prophets must painstakingly commit to equipping the body of Christ. That's part of our job.

THE ROLE OF THE PROPHET

Friends, now more than ever, the role of the prophet is essential not only for the church's witness in the world, but for within the church's own discipleship—especially in our post-pandemic culture. Way too many times, I hear prophetic voices denouncing rather than equipping, barking anger rather than embodying passion, crying about rather than weeping for, and drawing more attention to themselves rather than drawing people of faith—including themselves—to their knees in repentance. We prophets are forgetting who we are, what we're called to be, and why God has called us to the role in the first place. Prophets cannot be truly prophetic when they are physically and/or emotionally disengaged from the people of faith they are meant to build up.

Today, the prophetic role needs to communicate—in multiphasic ways—the values that Jesus himself espoused. Love, forgiveness, covenant, unity, justice, sacrifice (all of which are embedded in the Upper Room Discourse of John 13–17) form a discipleship "language" that is consistent with the prophetic call throughout the Scriptures, both Hebrew and New Testament alike. Learning that prophetic language comes first by immersion in real time—living out and living into the cultural expressions of community life under the leadership of Jesus Christ.

These values are seen most clearly in the mandates that Jesus brought to the table of fellowship with the Twelve. It was as they journeyed together, ate together, laughed together, learned together, prayed together, struggled together, and lived together that Jesus taught them the most basic qualities of life in the new community. And then he challenged them to live out those values with each other as a testimony to the world: "By this everyone will know that you are my disciples, if you have love for one another" (John 13:35).

All those values create a visual image of how the body of Christ, the church, is to be *different* from the rest of the world. The church thrives best when it is living out those values, representing Jesus in the world first by how it treats those within its fellowship. When conflict arises, for example, the church can represent itself differently than the human condition would warrant, so that its witness is consistent with the values of the One who gave his life for the sake of its mission, as well as with the sanctification processes wrought by the Spirit embedded in God's people.

Those values also create an environment within which it is safe for both leaders and followers to grieve, knowing that one's grief work is part of the discipleship process of not only the individual grieving, but of the community as well. Despite how we may feel in the moment, grief and loss are meant to be corporately shared experiences as we do life together. *All* of life.

GRIEF AS A MOSAIC

The problem with grief is that we humans tend to think and respond way too often within a linear, sequential worldview—when, in fact, reality calls us into seeing life and all its complexities more as a *mosaic*. The apostle Paul's words to the church in Corinth challenge us to look beyond our present circumstances into a reality that, at best, can be viewed through clouded lenses: "Now I know only in part; then I will know fully, even as I have been fully known" (1 Cor 13:12).

A mosaic is "a surface decoration made by inlaying small pieces of variously colored material to form pictures or patterns."[12] Most often, the best view of a mosaic is from a distance—so that one may see the full expression of the visual image that the composited tiles are to represent. For me, the mosaic is a powerful way of looking at different facets of the life of a disciple—from grief and trauma, to conflict and contrition, to forgiveness and reconciliation.

My theory is that when a "significant" event occurs—a death, a conflict, a trauma, an offense, a violation, a promotion, a move, a birth, a marriage, a divorce, an affair, a suicide, etc.—that event becomes imprinted on a "tile" in the greater masterpiece God is rendering of our life story. Our emotional response to that event creates a framework for how that event is catalogued and interpreted by our mind, coloring our experience of its

12. "Mosaic."

expression within our day-to-day life. The more "traumatic" the event, the more intense becomes the emotional reaction and the more focused we become on that event as defining our reality. Trauma—or more specifically, intense emotional pain—restricts our view to the individual tile representing that significant event, preventing us from seeing the larger picture of how that event contributes to our life story. Additionally, it blinds us from seeing how God could possibly redeem our pain.

In his seminal work on post-traumatic stress, *The Body Keeps the Score: Brain, Mind, and Body in the Healing of Trauma*, psychiatrist Dr. Bessel van der Kolk argues that within such a framework, traumas imprint themselves on the emotional part of our brains and influence how we view other situations that evoke similar emotional responses from us, regardless of whether such situations warrant it.[13]

That means that, whether within our individual lives or within the corporate life of an organization, traumas embedded in our experience will predicate an automated reaction that can influence how that organization will handle other stressors—including the losses resulting from leadership initiatives regardless of whether those initiatives are perceived as positive or negative.

In my field of conflict leadership, for example, that means that in any given conflict situation, participants' reactions may be complicated by their past experiences of previous (and probably unrelated) trauma, emotional pain, grief, and fear of abandonment, as they influence the present situation. In other words, in our congregations and organizations right now, there are people who are poised to react negatively to any conflict—or any change—that acts as a "trigger" to their past experiences of pain and trauma.

Our response as leaders, therefore, must be fluid, utilizing all the functions of our pastoral role to navigate through the individual and corporate layers of what can be unresolved, masked, traumatic, institutional, or generational grief.[14] This is especially true for those prophet-leaders among us who are compelled to step into situations of injustice—mediating and moderating emotions that often can be acrimonious as they represent the pain of those who are oppressed.

---

13. See van der Kolk, *Body Keeps Score*, 1–3, 21–23, 45–46.

14. Ross and Nisbett, *Person and Situation*, offer an excellent perspective on situational leadership consistent with this premise.

And guess what—all the above scenarios apply as well to every one of us leaders.

As we proactively empower a mosaic view of our life—and our life together within community—we nurture a communal perspective of the redemptive capacity of God for all experiences in the lives of Jesus's followers, both individual and corporate: "God never wastes a hurt."[15] For Jesus followers, the Lord reframes our experiences of brokenness, inviting us both to trust his redemptive work on our behalf, as well as to learn how to referee our responses to our own feelings of loss for the sake of the greater mission.

As the leaders go, so goes the organization. Notice "leaders" is plural. Even our leadership is meant to be done in community. Teams hold one another accountable for both personal and corporate spiritual formation and growth.

Everything is about mentoring disciples. Nothing is wasted. Even our personal experiences of loss play a role within God's compassionate spiritual formation of us as individuals, as well as a larger congregation of believers and organizations led by persons of faith. And those experiences, processed with honesty, increase our capacity to lead our organizations with integrity.

So, as leaders, how do we engage that mosaic from within our own experiences of loss? By grasping what the biblical prophets had—a glimpse of the prophetic vision of God's bigger plan that ultimately would take us to the cross of Jesus Christ. But how will that help us through the next phase of our grief—the season of anger, resentment, and bitterness that threatens to shape our life story in response to our loss? Let's ask the prophetess, Anna, within the context of what she learned.

---

15. See Reeve, *God Never Wastes*. I base the principle on his basic premise.

A Prophet in Time: Anna

"Blessed are you, Adonai, Ruler of the universe, who has renewed me with a good night's sleep and given me the gift of a new day."

Anna woke before dawn, as was typical for her these days. Sliding her feet gently out of the blanket and pushing herself up with her elbow, she sat at the side of her bed and said her morning prayers the same way her abba, Phaneul, had taught her back when she was a child. It was the first thing she did every morning, without fail.

It was not typical back then for a father to give such detailed religious instruction to a daughter. That was a mother's role. But her father saw a passion in Anna, a drive that inspired him. Certainly, he had his hands full with Anna's five brothers. Most days, keeping them occupied so that they would not overwhelm their mother was a full-time job. But Anna . . . Anna was his little girl. Their only girl. And she had her abba wrapped around her little finger. Plus, she was just plain smart. Nothing passed by Anna unnoticed. She saw the smallest details and asked the most insightful questions. Her intelligence, second only to her charisma, consistently made him smile with pride.

Anna's ima, her mother, on the other hand, was quicker to remind her to set the table or clear the dishes, which Anna did with great haste so that she could find herself at her abba's feet listening as he retold the great stories of the faith to her brothers and cousins after supper. She was uniquely drawn to the stories, captivated by the greater things Adonai had in mind for Israel.

"Adonai has something great in store for you, my daughter," Phaneul had said many a night as he tucked her into bed, planting a kiss on her forehead. "You wait and see."

In truth, her ima saw it too—this passion, this special anointing for the things of Adonai. Anna would catch her smiling from the doorway to her room every so often as her abba said his evening's goodnight.

"New, indeed, is your mercy, Adonai, every morning, for great is your faithfulness." Anna stretched, as much as her frail body would allow her to, stood up, and, shuffling a bit, made her way into the kitchen area of her small quarters. She gazed out the window and noticed the slight change in the color of the sky as nighttime was transitioning into morning. Already she could see activity beginning near the temple gates. Soon, all of Jerusalem would be busy with the activities of both faith and marketplace—people coming to do their religious obligations, and having to purchase the appropriate sheep, goats, oxen, turtledoves, or pigeons necessary to do so.

She could still pick out the pungent smells of burnt animal flesh that lingered in the air and seemed to cling to the fabrics that she used to cover her windows, a nasty by-product of living so close to the temple courtyards. She much preferred the more pleasant scents of the *qetoret*, the incense offerings burned by the priests every morning and evening, the smells of which always transported her back in time to when she first came to Jerusalem as a child with her abba and ima.

Anna picked up a little clay jar that sat on the window ledge. It contained a small sampling of the *qetoret* given to her eight years prior as a thank you from Caleb, the assistant to the high priest that year. Anna had helped the young man interpret a particularly difficult passage from the Torah before he had to give a report to his mentor. The gift was not necessary, of course, for she loved being asked by students to interpret Adonai's word. But truly she treasured this gift. She lifted its hand-formed lid, and carefully and slowly took a gentle whiff of its contents. The combination of spices was rich, sweet, and pleasant. It was the frankincense and coriander, in particular, that immediately reclaimed her morning senses and took her back to a happier time . . .

"You like those smells, my daughter?" her abba had asked her on one of their morning walks through the Jerusalem side streets.

"Yes, Abba, very much! It smells . . . sweet!"

"Ahh, yes!" he chuckled in response. "That is the smell of our prayers!"

"Our prayers, Abba?"

"Yes, my Anna. That is the sweet aroma of our prayers to Adonai. You remember your psalms, don't you? . . . When King David said, 'Let my prayer be counted as incense before you, and the lifting up of my hands as an evening sacrifice.'"[1]

Anna nodded, as she gazed into her abba's smiling face.

"I love that image, don't you?" he asked brightly, as they continued their walk. "It reminds me that even when words fail me and I don't know what specifically to pray, the incense prays for me. Anna, always remember that in good times and in bad, Adonai simply loves the sweetness of our being here and trusting in his goodness. Whenever you are struggling with something, just come to the temple courtyard and smell the air. At least—when the priests are offering the *qetoret!*" They laughed. "I especially love the frankincense and coriander, don't you?" He paused briefly, and then added, as he squiggled up his nose, "And . . . it also covers over the not-so-good smells of the animal sacrifices, don't you think?"

Anna's attention was brought back by the sounds in the outer courtyard—tables being moved into place and two men arguing with each other. Other merchants, too, were beginning to arrive, setting up their stands in the Court of the Gentiles so that they might sell their products to the pilgrims and visitors. Notoriously, there would be many who would be taking advantage of the newcomers with outlandishly high prices. An embarrassment to all Israel, she thought.

"Tsk!" It came out of her before she realized it. She did not want to start the day with sarcasm. Too many of the past eighty-four years' worth of days did, as the contrast of what the people of faith were called to be doing clashed with what they were actually doing.

"Today is going to be different, Adonai. Yes, today is going to be different. I can feel it. You told me to look for it—the sign of your promise. You didn't tell me when, though, but . . . " she chuckled to herself, "that would make the days less exciting, now wouldn't it? I've watched for your sign every day for decades. Perhaps it's going to be today. Yes, perhaps it's going to be today. Yes, the *hesed* of the Lord never ceases, Adonai's mercies never come to an end."

Anna had been stationing herself at the same spot in the temple courts for decades. It was her spot—and anyone worth their salt in Jerusalem, even the high priest himself (no matter which high priest it was at the time), knew enough not to challenge her spot. Not that she was a guardian of her position, mind you. Nor would any high priest ever vie for her place in the Court of the Women, for goodness' sake. Rather, it was out of deep respect

1. Ps 141:2.

that people deferred to her. You see, they all knew her story. They knew that Adonai spoke to her. And they knew that she spoke for Adonai.

Many, especially among the women, even called her a prophet—or prophetess—of the Most High. She really didn't care much for titles. At her age, she had seen plenty of kings, priests, and prophets who did not live up to their titles. For her, the evidence was in the fruit that people bore with their lives. Did people listen to Adonai, or did they just bicker about what Adonai "probably meant"? That was her plumbline. Regardless, her long tenure in the temple brought her great respect. So, when Anna spoke Adonai's messages, which, publicly, was not all that often, people listened to what she had to say.

From her spot just inside the Ezrat HaNashim, nearest to Solomon's Porch, Anna could see the various activities of people coming and going. Her experienced eyes still could identify from a great distance both people she knew and those she was sure were newcomers to Jerusalem. While she prayed—which was on and off all day and evening—those eyes scanned the courtyard, looking at each of the gates, waiting for any direction from Adonai. She liked to think of herself as being on a mission for Adonai.

On any given day, it was quite common for her to see young couples coming in for the appropriate rituals of purification and the presentations of their firstborn sons. Anna would smile, seeing their pride mixed with fear as they took their tentative steps through the outer courtyards, along with their requisite rituals, and then into the Court of the Women—their final destination, at least for the young women. She had seen that look of anxiety so many times over the years. She was genuinely overjoyed for them. And yet, there was a part of her heart that was sad—a deeply buried, but not forgotten part.

In those moments, she would often remember Aaron—her Aaron. Betrothed at a very early age, she and Aaron were the best of friends before they were destined to be husband and wife. When it came time to marry, both sets of parents threw an amazing wedding feast that kept the village talking for months. Yet, those *mazel tov* exclamations eventually turned into gossipy whispers: "So, why are there no children yet?" and "What are they waiting for?" They really had no clue as to how desperate Anna and Aaron were for children—how brokenhearted Anna had been that she could not provide a child for her husband. Aaron would never say anything, but she saw his expressions of inner pain when his friends or coworkers would make comments. She prayed agonizing prayers, asking Adonai for favor.

Favor. That's what her name meant, after all. Would Adonai not want them to have a child?

Then the unthinkable happened. An accident so terrible. Aaron, her Aaron, her husband of only seven years, was gone.

"You'll get married again, Anna," her mother had said after several months of seeing her daughter weeping in the darkened corners of her room. "There'll be plenty of time for you to find love again. And . . ." thinking that she was being helpful, ". . . to give me some grandchildren!"

But Anna had made the decision after Aaron's burial that she would not marry again. Whether it was from her grief at having lost Aaron, or a growing bitterness of never having had a child with the man she loved so much, she pushed off her personal happiness, believing that her life seemed better suited for solitude. Instead, she would spend the rest of her days at the temple, searching in prayer for the answers that would explain her grief, that would somehow redeem her pain.

And when the words of her grief failed her in prayer, perhaps the incense would pray for her instead.

Over the ensuing years, she never heard the answers she had longed for. Gradually, however, her prayers began to shift. Being at the temple eventually made her feel more at peace with Adonai, less angry and no longer bitter. Watching and listening to everything going on about her, she soon felt the urge to pray more specifically for what Adonai had in mind for the people of Israel. In fact, it genuinely burdened her soul. As the priests would read from the Torah, and as the cantors would chant the beautiful, rhythmic words of the psalms, her heart felt drawn toward the day when Messiah would come, when Adonai would finally redeem Israel. It had to be soon. God was about to do something new. She just knew it. She could feel it. She *heard* the rumblings inside her soul. It was as she had imagined labor pains would have felt like—just at the onset of new birth. So, she waited . . . and listened . . . and watched. For years.

People indeed called her a prophet, and maybe that was so. But for Anna, it was simpler than that. For her, it seemed as if she just understood Adonai's word when it was read. And she felt certain, by this Voice inside her, that she seemed to know how to apply that word to the situations before her. Over the years, people would come to her for advice, and she would instruct them from the many passages of the Torah that she had memorized since the days that her abba had taught her. Even some of the younger priests, like Caleb, would come during their evening strolls

A Prophet in Time: Anna

between courtyards and ask for her interpretations of some of the more challenging passages. This always made her smile since she knew that these young priests would eventually pass on what she had said to the priests further up the chain of command.

Fundamentally, she just saw herself as a listener—someone who had one ear to what was going on around her, and the other tuned specifically to that Voice that now had become so intimately familiar.

In fact, it was that Voice that now was interrupting her prayers.

"Now, Anna! It's time! Look!"

Long trusting that Voice, Anna lifted her face from her open-palmed hands—her preferred posture for praying—and immediately began scanning the courtyard. It was still midmorning, and the Court of the Women was filled with people who had just finished the *shacharit*, the first hour of prayer, making it difficult to pinpoint exactly what the Voice was wanting her to see. But then, in the middle of the crowd, she spied Simeon, her longtime friend, standing in front of a young couple. Even from this distance she could see Simeon raising his hand to his mouth as if catching himself in surprise and then suddenly lifting both arms in the air as if praising Adonai.

"Go!" the Voice commanded deep within her. Standing with an energy that she had not felt in years, she made her way across the courtyard and through the crowds, never taking her eyes off the child that she now saw cradled in the arms of its mother. Adrenalin was pushing her forward, making her heart pound in her chest.

As she arrived, Anna saw Simeon's face. It was aglow with wonder and a joy she had never seen on him before. Even as she looked at the child, she knew—she *knew*—that this was the Child of the Promise. This was the One who would redeem Israel. This was the One that she had waited for these past decades—through a lifetime of prayers. Anna saw that her reaction and that of Simeon were confusing the young parents. Their faces showed a mixture of protective uncertainty and awe at what was happening in front of them.

At once, Simeon took the child in his arms and began to praise Adonai, exclaiming that his eyes had seen Adonai's salvation, long prepared in the presence of all peoples. He even began to prophesy that this child was meant to be a light for revelation to the gentiles and for the glory of Israel. It was then, as Simeon was giving the child back to his mother, that he said something that deeply caught Anna, stirring her spirit with a deep sorrow, and yet a matchless joy at its wonder and truth: "This child is destined for the falling and the rising of many in Israel, and to be a sign that will be opposed so that the inner thoughts of many will be revealed." And then looking directly at the child's mother, Simeon added, quietly, knowingly: "And a sword will pierce your own soul too."[2]

There was so much truth in what Simeon had said, she knew it. And she knew that the Voice had directed her here for such a time as this. She, too, lifted her praise to Adonai, reciting many of the verses of the *Hallel* by heart, acknowledging the long-awaited time of redemption that had come at last.

A crowd began to form around them wondering what the commotion was about. Immediately in the Spirit, Anna began to tell those who gathered all about this child, this wonderful, beautiful child, and how Adonai was about to do a great thing, how Adonai had given birth to a new day for Israel . . . and for the world.

Long after the young couple had gone, Anna continued to repeat the story over and over to anyone who came near. She herself felt reborn with an energy—a life—that she had not known in years. Adonai had allowed her to see with her own eyes what the Voice had hinted at decades prior. And she got to tell so many people about Adonai's larger plan—a plan that she had heard years back, while sitting at her abba's feet.

Redemption. Finally, what Isaiah had said would come true: "The people who walked in darkness have seen a great light; those who lived in a land of deep darkness—on them light has shined."[3]

She had seen that Light. It was a Child. Adonai's Promise.

Israel would finally be redeemed.

And so would her own grief.

It was then that she noticed the evening incense aromas filling the air—especially the frankincense and coriander. Prayers had been heard. Adonai would be pleased.

---

2. Luke 2:28–32.

3. Isa 9:2.

2

Anger

Forgiveness is God's "perfect" response to loss.

At that moment she came, and began to praise God and to speak about the child to all who were looking for the redemption of Jerusalem.

—Luke 2:38

THREE VERSES. THAT'S ALL we have of Anna's story in the entire New Testament. Yet, those three verses remind us that behind every face there's a story.

Three verses. A single tile in the mosaic's metanarrative of what God was—and is—doing through Jesus Christ for the redemption of humanity. And if we pull back the curtain and investigate the behind-the-scenes story line of Anna's life—which, for us, requires speculation and extrapolation, at best—we discover that those three verses reflect at least eighty-four years of heartache and hope, of loss and discovery, and of grief and grace.

What was it that made Anna "exit" her expected path in life and turn toward a ministry within the walls of the temple courtyards? What unresolved questions, if any, burdened her enough to keep her "praying and fasting" day and night for decades? What layers of grief did she have to process through to negotiate with God in the healing of her pain?

With her marriage ending abruptly, and no scriptural evidence of her ever having had children, how would she have coped with the vacuous feelings that, I imagine, she may have felt? Was she angry at her husband for dying? With God for taking him? With herself for missed opportunities?

And from her intentional searching of the heart of God, what did she discern of God's mosaic plan that would both give her the credentials of a prophetess within the constructs of temple life, as well as get her passions revved up enough to become Jesus's very first evangelist?

Anger. Resentment. Regret. Bitterness. Were they a part of Anna's grief story as they might have been for ours?

Anna's prophetic ministry has a context—a context that comes to us mostly hidden. Yet, she is fully human, seasoned and tempered by spending decades within the crucible of God's redemptive, reconciling grace. Within just three verses we discover that her loss, her grief, her pain, her healing, her leadership—and her prophetic voice—mattered.

It is into that crucible that every leader must go to spar with the God who gives and takes away (Job 1:21). Because our loss, grief, pain, healing, leadership—and prophetic voice—matter too.

As with Anna, we too must allow our losses to be reframed within the umbrella of redemption—by a process that we know as forgiveness. For God the Redeemer never wastes a hurt.

And neither should we.

FORGIVENESS: GOD'S COUNTER TO THE ANGER OF LOSS

We place a lot of expectations onto forgiveness. We expect it to heal relationships, restore intimacy, equalize power, confront prior iniquities and inequities, relinquish painful memories, and restore everything to our view of a more perfect world. We embody it when we need it, withhold it when we are still hurting from what someone posted about us on social media, preach it when we need to posture "Christian values," avoid it when it calls us to accountability, and forget it when it prevents us from getting our own way.

Been there. Done that. Even as I'm sure you have too.

The truth, however, is that forgiveness is a very fragile thing. It's a delicate process of self-discovery as we finally emerge out of our seasons of denial, push past the layers of pain and anger that threaten to redefine our life story, and discover that intrinsically, we are just like the person or persons that have offended us.[1]

---

1. Patton, *Forgiveness Possible?*, 16.

And because of that, forgiveness scares us. So much so that many of us avoid it, even though we understand how vital it is for our relational well-being, even though we've heard since the days of Sunday school that Jesus mandates it, even though we know that our witness depends on it. Many of us live our lives under the impression that forgiveness means weakness. As leaders, we don't want to feel vulnerable. For some of us, that scares us more than our pain.

And, quite honestly, some of us have a need to hold onto our anger. (More on that in just a moment.)

We would prefer to address forgiveness on our own terms—giving us some sense of personal control over our outcomes, biding our time for the days of payback, and perhaps even "forgetting" the offense because we can't face the harder ramifications of living with pain or loving through loss. We might even let ourselves "off the hook," while simultaneously holding higher standards against those who hurt us.

The problem is that for forgiveness to be genuine, something must die. Specifically, something *inside us* must die. Whether it's our need to be right, our false sense of importance, our need for personal validation, or our bruised-ego need to be seen as the victim—it needs to be sacrificed at the altar of grace for forgiveness to overshadow our pain.

In fact, forgiveness stands at the crossroads of judgment and grace as God's powerful secret weapon. It slays the prideful and bolsters the humble as it tears down our false sense of security while it brandishes its blade of unmerited grace. In simple terms, it is the grand, divine counteroffer to loss, thereby forever linking it to the redemptive processes of grief.

LOSS AND FORGIVENESS

As I shared previously, grief is our normal human response to change. The more intense the change is, the more intense the grief response will be. When during our daily lives, significant changes occur—the death of a loved one, the betrayal of a friend, the ending of a marriage, the loss of a job, the failure of a project, a move to a new town—it is common for us to feel anxious, or even violated, that our once secure, seemingly "normal" world has been invaded or altered, confronting us with the need to process and adjust, whether or not we want to.

Large or small, every act of said "violation," therefore, produces loss—a loss of trust, a loss of intimacy, a loss of innocence, a loss of (perceived) power, a loss to one's identity, a loss of security, a loss of hope, a loss of stability, a loss of physical, emotional, spiritual, or cognitive well-being, even a loss of social connections,[2] to name just a few. The key word in this list is *loss*. Change produces loss. And loss expects a response—something, anything, that will realign us to our sense of normalcy. Forgiveness is that equalizer. Therefore, our understanding of forgiveness—the central fixture of our Christian faith—must intermingle with our theology of grief. Our leadership depends on its integration.

In his book, *Helping People Forgive*, author and pastor David Augsburger writes, "Grief work is a process of multiple journeys into memory. In grieving, one leaves the 'here and now' and returns to the 'there and then' because the emotional world has stopped its forward movement in frozen attachment to the ice-cold reality of loss. The many journeys backward—telling and retelling parts of the story—slowly thaws what has been frozen and at last melts the ice attachment. In grief work, the speech is predominantly past tense, the stance is backward, until the bond with the loss breaks. The sudden appearance of future-tense verbs is familiar to grief counselors as the sign of turning outward, turning forward, returning to life. Forgrieving, in parallel process, requires this revisiting of the past, reworking of the injury, and rebuilding of the loss through reframing and reinterpreting its meaning."[3]

Augsburger's term "forgrieving," one that he himself coined, describes the intimate link between forgiveness and grief. For him, the emotional processes of the one are identical to those of the other.

I agree. Yet, I'd like to take Augsburger's theory one step further—into an even larger mosaic perspective. For me, from a human perspective, forgiveness is a *transitional* process rather than a *transactional* one—meaning that it's something that is discovered enroute to a newly defined relationship, rather than a business arrangement brokered in the exchange of services. And if we're to live and lead forgiveness well within God's grander mosaic, then we need to understand this transitional process from within its "perfect" world. Let me explain.

---

2. Augsburger, *Helping People Forgive*, 130–45.
3. Augsburger, *Helping People Forgive*, 68.

THE PERFECT-TENSE EXPERIENCE

In the grammar of ancient Greek, which was the primary language of the New Testament canon, the "perfect tense" is used to convey an event that has occurred in the past, but the effects of which continue to impact the present.[4] I call it "a past tense with a kick into the present." Here are a few examples of the perfect tense:

- "James has been waiting since the third hour." (Meaning that he's still waiting.)
- "Anna has gone to the temple to pray." (Meaning that she's still there.)
- "The Zebedee brothers have shopped in this market for years." (Meaning that they have an ongoing connection with the market.)
- "Lydia has been reading ever since she arrived at her aunt's home." (Meaning that Lydia is still reading since her arrival.)

In addition to its grammatical importance, I believe that the perfect tense has broader, more metaphoric applications that will assist us in understanding loss, grief, and leadership from the mosaic perspective. For example, one of the best illustrations of this "perfect tense" concept for followers of Jesus can be found within the church's liturgy of Holy Communion—specifically, with our understanding of the ancient Greek word *anamnesis*, "remembrance," and its theological implications.

Within many of our liturgies and practices of Communion, the leader invites us to break bread "in remembrance of" Jesus's death by recalling the experiences of the disciples in their last hours with Jesus:

> On the night in which he gave himself up for us, Jesus took bread, gave thanks, broke the bread, gave it to his disciples, and said, "Take, eat; this is my body which is given for you. Do this in remembrance of me." When the supper was over, Jesus took the cup, gave thanks, gave it to his disciples, and said, "Drink from this, all of you; this is my blood of the new covenant, poured out for you and for many for the forgiveness of sins. Do this, as often as you drink it, in remembrance of me."[5]

---

4. Crosby and Schaeffer, *Introduction to Greek*, 173.

5. As illustration, this liturgy was adapted from United Methodist Church, "Service of Word."

Typically, these words are preceded by an invitation to repent along with a prayer of confession consistent with our faith perspective—opportunities to connect oneself to the reason that Jesus died on the cross.

By remembering *together*, which the sacrament's liturgy supports, the community that gathers at the table is invited to "reparticipate" in the salvific and sanctifying ramifications of a single event that *had already occurred* in the past—Jesus's death on the cross. Simultaneously, that past event then "recalls" participants to remember who they are as Christ-followers *today*, and until he returns. The crucifixion and death of Jesus, intimately connected for believers as a single event in time, becomes a perfect-tense experience—an event that occurred in the past, yet the effects of which continue into the present.

As followers of Jesus, our ability to forgive today, therefore, comes when, over time, we remember that we ourselves have been forgiven—specifically, by a single event that had occurred previously, and by a man who lived and died over two thousand years before we were born.

The apostle Paul's second letter to the Corinthian church captures both this perfect-tense concept as well as its place within the larger divine mosaic:

> From now on, therefore, we regard no one from a human point of view; even though we once knew Christ from a human point of view, we know him no longer in that way. So if anyone is in Christ, there is a new creation: everything old has passed away; see, everything has become new! All this is from God, who reconciled us to himself through Christ, and has given us the ministry of reconciliation; that is, in Christ God was reconciling the world to himself, not counting their trespasses against them, and entrusting the message of reconciliation to us. So we are ambassadors for Christ, since God is making his appeal through us; we entreat you on behalf of Christ, be reconciled to God. For our sake he made him to be sin who knew no sin, so that in him we might become the righteousness of God. (2 Cor 5:16–21)

For Paul and for us, the concept of forgiveness is to be understood as part of the rubric of this "anamnesis community,"[6] the "called out" community of

---

6. Enright, "Psychological Science," 23. Enright introduces the concept of "the Forgiving Community," which he defines as "a system-wide effort to make forgiveness a conscious and deliberate part of human relations through: discussion, practice, mutual support, and the preservation of forgiveness across time in any group that wishes to cultivate and perfect this virtue (alongside justice and all other virtues)." In my book, I posit that the Christian church, by definition, should be such a community—utilizing a theological framework rooted in the cross-resurrection "perfect-tense events." I suggest

faith.⁷ Within the "perfect" world, grief, loss, and forgiveness become corporately shared events by virtue of our communion together. Our experiences of violation, as well as our acts of forgiveness, therefore, are to be seen as part of the unfolding, and fully redemptive, mosaic of the divine mission.

A COMMUNITY THAT REMEMBERS

When the people of faith identify themselves by the perfect-tense event of the crucifixion—as well as the subsequent perfect-tense event of the resurrection of Jesus—according to Paul, a "new creation" occurs providing yet another perfect-tense event for each individual, as well as for the community of gathered believers (2 Cor 5:17). That new creation has ramifications on how believers—both new and longer-tenured—are to live their lives from that moment forward. Through Christ, they become agents of love and forgiveness *because* they have been loved and forgiven, as demonstrated by the cross and the empty tomb.

Within such an anamnesis community, forgiveness, therefore, is rooted in our remembering who we are in Christ, what God *already* accomplished in Jesus's death on the cross, and that Jesus will be coming again to "reconcile the world to himself" (2 Cor 5:19). Paul reminds the Corinthian believers, and us, that our present suffering has been, and will be, redeemed by the One who suffered for the sins of humanity on the cross. Because of Jesus, perfect-tense redemption empowers present- (and future-) tense interpersonal forgiveness.⁸

Easy, right? Not so fast.

---

an application process based on eschatological and missiological ramifications, rather than an individual (or corporate) psychodynamic rationale.

7. Marty, "Ethos of Christian Forgiveness," 22.

8. For an interesting international take on this topic, see Jackson, "Reconnecting the Rhetoric," 55–56. In arguing for a more sound, biblical response to the betrayals and forgiveness cycles within Northern Ireland, theologian and activist Jackson calls for a deeper understanding of interpersonal forgiveness by drawing the community of faith to remember what Jesus did on the cross: "Even though this memory is descriptive of an historical event in the life of Jesus and is absolutely unrepeatable in any form, it has a continuing dynamic and transformative impact on life as we live it." Within his own context, Jackson rightly posits that "reconciliation, atonement and memory respect events as what happens in time; they do not pretend that nothing has happened or that what happened was not intentional; however, they manifest the God-given and God-driven imperative to transcend and transform the past in the present for the sake of the future."

FORGIVE AND REMEMBER

Certainly, the act of gathering for the sacrament of Communion reminds us that, as followers of Jesus, we are *not* to be a people that "forgive and forget," but rather, a people that "remember and forgive." Yet, as much as *anamnesis* is essential within the perfect-tense experience of forgiveness, not all remembering feels redemptive for the Christian believer. In his book, *The Road Home: A Guided Journey to Church Forgiveness and Reconciliation*, Darrell Puls exposes the fact that within the fully human church of Jesus Christ, "we cannot forgive and forget, and so we remember and hate, replaying everything over and over in an endless cycle, furtively licking at the elusive, sweet taste of imagined revenge like a sun-scorched desert wanderer gingerly trying to lick morning dew from a cactus. We harbor our pain, holding it close and nurturing it, for sometimes it is all we have. Or, tired and defeated from too much humiliation and hurt, we sink into the maw of depression where life loses its color and flavor, a barren gray place without hope or joy."[9]

The reality, according to Puls, is that "we cannot confront the past without remembering it; we cannot lessen the pain without remembering what it was; we cannot leave it behind without remembering what it is that we leave."[10]

Therefore, forgiveness within an anamnesis community can be redemptive only when the believer engages the pain of the relational injury with honesty and integrity—and then grieves the losses that such injury has produced. While forgiveness is rooted in a single event in the past, the effects of that cross-event inaugurate a *transition* in the believer—a process of moving through the phases necessary to bring them to a place of healing and restoration.

Augsburger, once again, clarifies that "we do not forget when we forgive, but the meaning of the memory changes. . . . Forgiving is active and aware; it is recognizing the injury, owning the pain, and reaching out to reframe, re-create, restore, reconstruct, rebuild, reopen what can be opened."[11] For the relationships that are important to us, and even for our own personal well-being when offense is done by those who are not relationally connected to us, we cannot disengage from the painful realities and

---

9. Puls, *Road Home*, 3–4.
10. Puls, *Road Home*, 126.
11. Augsburger, *Helping People Forgive*, 28.

ramifications of our violations. Whether we forgive or not, those violations produce loss; and our losses must be acknowledged and grieved for healing to occur. Forgiveness is neither ignoring an offense nor forgetting an offense. Rather, it can be seen as what my good friend and psychologist Dr. Jesse Gill calls a "divine gift to set you free and help you to move through your grief and pain."[12] We cannot "release" a person from a "debt" that they owe us if we do not acknowledge the debt that has been accrued.[13]

Joseph's Story

Within Judaism, the paragon for the Jewish praxis of forgiveness is Joseph,[14] whose story in Gen 37–50 not only embodies the divine epitome of undeserved grace, but also fully illustrates a mosaic interpretation of his circumstances: "I am your brother Joseph, whom you sold into Egypt. And now do not be distressed, or angry with yourselves, because you sold me here; *for God sent me before you* to preserve life. For the famine has been in the land these two years; and there are five more years in which there will be neither ploughing nor harvest. *God sent me before you* to preserve for you a remnant on earth, and to keep alive for you many survivors. So it was *not you who sent me here, but God.*" (Gen 45:4–8, italics mine).

Yet, after Jacob dies, Joseph's brothers once again feel the potent fear that Joseph's forgiveness was somehow conditional. Joseph must reassert his affirmation of forgiveness years after their reconciliation had been accomplished: "But Joseph said to them, 'Do not be afraid! Am I in the place of God? Even though you intended to do harm to me, God intended it for good, in order to preserve a numerous people, *as he is doing today*" (Gen 50:19–20, italics mine).

Depending on the nature and intensity of one's experiences of grief, the emotional scars of such imprinted memories can become embedded within the communal history of that person's family, church, or tribe thereby impacting the culture of that community and challenging its identity as a "forgiving-forgiven people."[15] Significant interpersonal violations of those

12. Gill, *Face to Face*, 255.

13. Myers, "Jesus' New Economy."

14. For an interesting take on this, see McConville, "Forgiveness as Private and Public," 635.

15. Augsburger, *Helping People Forgive*, 117. See also Murray, "Therapeutic Use of Forgiveness," 188, and his intriguing research on using forgiveness processes within

within anamnesis communities—especially when left unexamined and unforgiven—in their own right can become perfect-tense experiences for the community as well—single events of past violation that implicate future generations within its ramifications, whether positively or negatively.

FORGIVING BY GRIEVING

While there are several Greek words in the New Testament that may be translated as "forgive," one of the primary words used, *aphiemi*, is most intriguing to me. Formed by the combination of two words, *apo*, which means "from," and *hiemi*, which means "to send," it typically is translated as "to release"—or more specifically, to release someone from responsibility for the offense they have perpetrated or the debt that they have accrued.[16] That "releasing" is a *transitional* process, sometimes long in duration, by which one comes to terms with the offense—and all of the feelings related to it.[17]

I believe that such a process of release is the same process one experiences in grief work—for an act of "offense" officiates the experience of loss, whether perceived or actual. To forgive, therefore, one must grieve the loss that such an offense has instigated, allowing its past-tense remembrance to reorient the forgiver into a new relationship with the forgiven—a relationship that is now informed by a learned response within the mosaic of their mutual story. In so doing, new boundaries are established in the relationship, trust progressively is restored (or clarified), and a new self-awareness is birthed—all because the offended individual chooses to move into their pain and loss, embracing the reality of their situation, grieving the ending of "what was" (e.g., the perceived internal and/or external security of the relationship, the intimacy dynamics of the relationship, one's own sense of "innocence" to the conflicts of others, etc.), and intentionally releasing the offender from any debt-claim they have over their victim's life.

Darrell Puls argues that forgiveness is a process that "requires a truthful examination and turning from the past that neither ignores past wrongs nor excuses them, that neither overlooks justice nor reduces justice to revenge, that insists on the humanity of opponents even in their commission of dehumanizing deeds, that values justice that restores above justice that destroys, and that restores trust through merciful justice and mutual

---

intergenerational healing.

16. Rye et al., "Religious Perspectives," 20.
17. Augsburger, *Caring Enough to Forgive*, 55.

restoration."[18] Additionally, I argue that such a "turning from the past" best mediates forgiveness, but only when we are able to view our present relational injury as part of the mosaic of God's redemptive work within our grander life-story.

In as much as our "present-tense" experiences of loss become perfect-tense experiences that produce ramifications for our future, we do not live outside of God's larger mosaic. Events within our daily lives can trigger reactions, memories of the loss or violation, and their associated emotional, physical, and/or psychological pain.[19] At present, our lives are an accumulation of past losses—both perpetrated and received. How those perfect-tense experiences influence present-tense well-being depends both on how those past events were grieved and processed, individually and within their anamnesis community, as well as how we have come to see ourselves as "equal" at the foot of the cross of Christ to the one who we perceive to be the perpetrator of our pain. By doing so, any act of forgiveness can become "a response of gratitude to a forgiving and gracious God."[20]

Grieved appropriately, individually as well as within one's community, forgiveness then becomes an outward and visible sign of an inward and spiritual grace, an experience that only God could mediate within a person's heart because only God could mediate it historically and globally in the perfect-tense experience of the crucifixion and resurrection of Jesus Christ. Thus, for the Christian, forgiveness is a "sacramental sign" that one is truly part of God's anamnesis community. One's relational injury is thus but one "tile" in the larger mosaic of God's redemptive work. For the believer in Jesus, a decision (or series of decisions) "to release internal feelings of anger, resentment, fear, and the desire for revenge against someone who has harmed us" is a decision to participate in the greater mission of the new community of Jesus followers.[21] Such a perspective can help initiate feelings of release—or even empathy—towards one's offender,[22] giving the offended the spiritual strength to "abandon a sense of blame and replacing that feeling with compassion; it is unconditional and does not rely on the offender's response."[23]

18. Puls, *Road Home*, 43.
19. Fife et al., "Facilitating Forgiveness," 360.
20. McMinn et al., "Forgiveness and Prayer," 102.
21. Puls, *Road Home*, 43.
22. Fife et al., "Facilitating Forgiveness," 355.
23. Menahem and Love, "Forgiveness in Psychotherapy," 829.

Yet, it may take some time to do so—since some issues of violation are incredibly painful and deeply felt. And, of course, we must be willing.

BEYOND A THERAPEUTIC COMMUNITY

There are many reasons why we might want to withhold forgiveness from someone who has hurt us. Often, our pain runs deep. Especially when God is the one we classify as the "offender." Our trust of the offender has been violated—perhaps even beyond repair. In fact, the offender may not have showed any sense of remorse or acknowledgment of the hurt they inflicted on us. Maybe all we received from our offender in response to our pain is silence. In our opinion, they may not deserve to be forgiven. We may want them to suffer in the isolation of their guilt, that is, if they even acknowledge their guilt. They may not even care that their words or actions caused us pain.

In the grief of our violations, we often draw others in to take "our side," to validate our feelings, or to justify our "righteous" cause. Some, perhaps many, of our experiences of violation impact the larger communities within which we connect—family, friendship circles, church, workplace. As our pain radiates out into those circles, the community is affected. Lines of affiliation are drawn. Relational loyalties may take place within emotional triangles as others begin to react to emotional pains that are not their own. Victimization is sometimes justified.

There indeed are many reasons why we might want to withhold forgiveness. Trust me, I've lived—and felt—many of them myself. Yet, there are at least two reasons *not* to withhold it.

Reason #1: Jesus Mandates It

The first reason is more obvious: Jesus mandates forgiveness. Certainly, it is a choice—even for those of us who are his followers (Matt 6:14–15). Yet, to be Jesus's follower requires that we live out his teaching, walk in his footsteps, and navigate ourselves to the cross where we discover our own need for forgiveness. Truly, I understand the difficult nature of that statement. There have been people in my life that, at times, make me want to forget that I am a follower of Jesus. I'm an Italian kid from New Jersey, after all. One of the many reasons that I'm not God is that there are people on my "offender list" that would no longer be here! But Jesus has called me "out of darkness" (1 Pet 2:9). He did that for you too. A decision to follow him must not ignore the whole point of his crucifixion. Forgiveness—no matter how you define it—is not based on worthiness. It's a choice to release someone from a debt that they owe us.

Reason #2: It Impacts Our Witness

The second reason not to withhold forgiveness is that whether we forgive or not impacts the witness of the church. As stated above, as followers of Jesus, we are not a people who live in isolation. Our choices impact community. But here's the blessing behind that challenge. Forgiving reminds us that those of us who are offended are not victims, but rather the ones with all the power. According to John's Gospel, after Jesus's resurrection, he appeared to the disciples, breathed on them the gift of the Holy Spirit, and then said, "If you forgive the sins of any, they *are forgiven* them; if you retain the sins of any, they *are retained*" (John 20:22–23, italics mine). The verbs "are forgiven" and "are retained," in Greek, are in the perfect tense. Post-resurrection, those disciples were given the Spirit as well as the authority to forgive or to withhold forgiveness. Talk about a test of power (more about that in chapter 4). Well, I believe that message came to the church by way of those disciples—specifically, to all on whom the Holy Spirit rests. By virtue of the cross of Christ, Jesus's followers are no longer to be bound by the category of "victim" when it comes to the issues of forgiveness. Jesus mandates forgiveness from his followers to remind them that they have an authority from the Holy Spirit to live differently than the world.

So, we need to learn how to be present with one another in our pain, in our losses, in our grief, while at the same time, setting limits on how that pain will be expressed outside of the arenas of the hurting relationship. Trauma, especially, is not easily healed. It takes time—sometimes a long time. Until forgiveness can work itself into and through the layers of trauma, our anger is self-protective, covering hidden pockets of fear and deeply scarred wounds. It serves an important purpose for us until we are ready to shed its protective coating. Until then we need to support one another, comfort one another, and counsel one another while we help one another to remember that there's a bigger mosaic that is affecting our discipleship under the God who never wastes anything.

This is hard stuff, for sure. Especially when our pain is directed at God—when we perceive God to be the "violator." Yet, the principles are the same—although we may struggle at times with the concept of needing to "forgive" God. We must remember to engage the mosaic, however, with respect for the role that such suffering plays in our journey of trusting God when, in our "tiles" of violation, we may have felt God's absence more than God's presence. The storyline of the mosaic is usually not clear during the seasons of our losses—and definitely not in the traumatic moments of our violations. Honesty and compassion must walk together on this journey to rediscover hope.

Like Anna in my fictionalized rendition of her story, we may never understand the reasons for our losses, at least, this side of heaven. But denying ourselves, taking up our cross daily, and following Jesus (Luke 9:23) is ultimately what we signed up for. It is the entre point to the mosaic, uniting us with people like Job (Job 38:4–30) and Qoheleth (Eccl 2:1–6:9), along with the many witnesses to the faith over the course of two millennia who gave their lives to the divine mission without necessarily seeing the reasons for their suffering.

This is our role as prophet-leader. We are interpreters of the mosaic in the face of loss to provide hope for our mission.

INTEGRATING APPLICATIONS

As such, our role is to tell a larger story—God's story. This story is a glimpse at the divine mosaic that invites us to reorient our story into God's. At those intersections, our losses can be reframed as we realize that God never wastes a hurt. The prophetess Anna reminds us that to discover that mosaic we need to be "looking for the redemption" of God's people (Luke 2:38). As we are looking, watching, and waiting, we can connect with the heart of God's plan—a plan that draws people to the cross of Christ, the centerpiece of that redemption story. The cross invites us to view our lives as part of God's redemptive story, even as the apostle Paul's words in Gal 2:20 become our own confession of faith as well: "I have been crucified with Christ; and it is no longer I who live, but it is Christ who lives in me. And the life I now live in the flesh I live by faith in the Son of God, who loved me and gave himself for me."

So, what does all this mean in practical terms for those of us who are leaders? What does it mean for the ministry within which we serve presently? Here, I present three implications and applications, describing what, in fact, "must die" for us to be the community known by its capacity to forgive:

- We need to teach forgiveness from a mosaic perspective—since we cannot hold people accountable to what we have not taught them
- We need to deconstruct the therapeutic mindset that our individual pain must be resolved before we can move forward on mission
- We need to model "missional empathy" within community—equipping our organizations on how to not only tolerate one another's pain, but use that pain to propel us forward on mission

Application #1: Teaching Forgiveness

First, despite the resurgence of forgiveness theories and self-help principles within our current culture today, and despite our uniquely redemptive heritage, Christians generally do not really know how to forgive. In fact, in my opinion, the way most Christians forgive looks no different from the way non-Christians forgive. Homiletically (and somewhat polemically) stated, many of us Christians follow Jesus only up to the Last Supper; we then skip over the cross and go directly to the empty tomb, preferring to be known as God's "resurrection people," yet without facing the agony of what it means to "die to self."

Indeed, to go to the cross within our own discipleship journey is to risk too much of our vulnerability and insecurity when it comes to our faith. We prefer to avoid grief all together, blame others for how we feel, keep relationships based on an intimacy that we define for ourselves, and hold others accountable rather than looking at the "plank in our own eye" (Matt 7:3–5).

To address this in our organizational contexts, we need to teach and model how to become a forgiving people within community—a community that cares. We need to begin to view ourselves less individualistically and more as part of a perfect-tense community that has a mandated role in the advancing of God's mission and seeing how the cross and the resurrection events of the past have sway over how we treat each other today. We need to relearn that we are citizens of the new community of Jesus followers first, before we are members of any other dominion, and therefore, how we forgive has ecclesiological, missiological, and eschatological implications.

Sadly, and most profoundly, the best illustration of what I'm talking about can be seen in the response of the Amish community to the school shooting in Nickel Mines, Lancaster County, Pennsylvania. In early October 2006, Charles Carl Roberts IV, in response to his own hardened, unforgiving heart and deep-rooted, unrelenting grief, took the lives of five young girls, significantly injured five other girls, and stole the sacred innocence of the remaining sixteen children (as well as the adults present in the classroom).[24] His actions, by definition of all humanity, were unforgiveable. Yet, forgiveness found him within a profound incarnational grace—despite the devastating evil that threatened the quilt-like fabric of the Amish faith community.

I remember it all too well. I have served as a pastor in Lancaster County, Pennsylvania, for over thirty-five years now and have driven through the Nickel Mines community many times over those years. The stark pall that subsequently covered this Amish community remained for quite some time as a post-traumatic blanket—alongside of yet another "quilt," covered not with the blood of innocent children, but with the blood of Jesus Christ. Side by side, one redeeming the other, both metaphorical blankets draped as memorials to a day that evil perpetrated—and yet God restored with hope. The hope came from the victim's families. Though grief-stricken themselves, their empathy and compassion toward Roberts's family (his wife and children, in particular) caused an entire community to act differently from the secular world of twenty-first-century cynical America. Instead of responding with litigation, they responded with a litany of forgiveness that bore testimony to the fact that the Amish live what they believe.

For those of us who regularly engage the Amish here in the "Bible-belt of the North," what impacted us most intensely in this situation was the powerful sense of grace proffered in that paradox of venues: the violation of innocent children occurred within a once-sacrosanct, one-room schoolhouse, out in the bucolic community of "God's country." The Amish community embodies a nonviolent, strict engagement of the biblical faith. They are unassuming, hardworking, diligent, and faithful—observing the self-protective and self-defining boundaries that have kept them in their simple lifestyle for generations. All of that was severely tested that horrific day.

The Amish passed the test.

While many in our modern world see forgiveness as a sign of weakness, especially in the face of traumatic violation, and most especially when that violation involves children, the Amish proved to us that forgiveness is founded on a deep-rooted confidence in the God who gave his all to forgive us. Compassion within forgiveness can only be offered when it is realized and personalized. There was no denial of their pain or loss, no denial of the

---

24. For a reflection of this story from the perspective of Charles Roberts's wife, see Roberts and Windle, *Forgiven: The Amish School Shooting*.

perpetrator's guilt, no cover-up of the dire nature of the act itself. Rather, walking into their pain, they chose to respond out of love to the "other victims" in this tragedy—the perpetrator's wife and children, who also were forever changed by his evil deeds.

This is the Amish way. They lived it with integrity. In doing so, they brought shame to the evil forces that thought they would win the day, as well as a challenge to a nation that seemed to have forgotten what it means to forgive.

The pain is still there though—not hidden, but out in front. Months after it was torn down in acknowledgment of their pain, the community gathered again to build a new school. The New Hope School now stands near where the old school once stood, decidedly different in appearance. Children play outside and learn inside. Hope defines the community again. Yet surrounding many of the Amish schools in the region are obvious wire fences and "No Trespassing" signs—to mark once again their boundary of privacy and the greater boundaries that promise to restore innocence. Such a marker calls us to the reality that true forgiveness remembers and learns.

The only way for the church to model this kind of self-giving love and forgiveness to the world is for us to practice it daily *among ourselves* within the anamnesis community.[25] Moving ourselves to the foot of the cross of Christ and discovering the perfect-tense equality of our mutual need for God's grace inaugurates empathy and compassion within us towards those who have offended us. Done daily, with intentionality, we become like the One whom we worship.

Application #2: Deconstructing the Therapeutic Mindset

Secondly, while Scripture clearly marks those who put their trust in Jesus as those who grieve, but not as those who have no hope (1 Thess 4:13), the church does not know how to face its own losses without fear. Indeed, that is quite human. Yet, for believers in Jesus Christ, loss still seems to have a defining "sting" (1 Cor 15:55) that prevents us from navigating through our inevitable losses. In our grief, we tend to focus on the "tile" event of our individual loss, rather than on the mosaic of our life-story and the God who redeems it. Certainly understandable, right? Pain is pain. We cope with it the best ways that we know how. Yet, we must be reminded that we serve a God who never wastes a hurt.

25. Enright, "Psychological Science," 27.

Unfortunately, especially here in the western hemisphere, we Christians have become spoiled by the "therapeutic sensibility" of our culture, becoming rather entitled and narcissistic in an age of apathy and minimal persecution.[26] Yet, for followers of Jesus who are defined by the cross and resurrection events of history, forgiveness demands a broader response.

We need to learn how to do authentic relationships—how to listen with love, engage with grace, and reconcile toward the advancing mission of God, not just to our own satisfaction. We need to challenge within ourselves and within our anamnesis community the long-tenured, highly reactive, overly sensitized view of ourselves as victims, rather than as those who are called to lose their life for Christ's sake to find life (Luke 9:23–25). Within his family systems perspective, psychiatrist and rabbi Edwin Friedman correctly argues that "making everyone sensitive to the sensitivities of others plays into the hands of those who feel powerless."[27] Darrell Puls also is correct when he writes, "Luke was very clear that to become a believer is to sacrifice ownership of the self to God and to each other. Most believers are willing to accept some shift in ownership of the self to God (at least partially), but few are willing to subordinate themselves to each other within the framework of the church."[28]

To address this, we need to use every funeral, every wedding (for even the positive events in our lives produce loss related to change), and every experience involving significant transition (e.g., a new sanctuary, a new worship schedule, an employee's separation, a merger, etc.) to underscore for our disciples-in-training the transitional nature of loss as well as its redemptive value within our life together. We need to equip our organizations with the hands-on, practical, in-the-field training of endurance, based on the principle of Rom 5:1–5: "But we also boast in our sufferings, knowing that suffering produces *endurance*, and endurance produces character, and character produces hope, and hope does not disappoint us, because God's love has been poured into our hearts through the Holy Spirit that has been given to us" (italics mine).

---

26. Augsburger, *Caring Enough to Forgive*, 104.

27. Friedman, *Failure of Nerve*, 71. This is not to say that there are not true "victims" on whom evil is perpetrated. I am referring here to the propensity within our culture to overly view ourselves as victims—and thereby constantly respond with litigation rather than love, inclusivity rather than accountability, and "cheap grace" rather than "costly grace," a concept first posited by Dietrich Bonhoeffer in his classic *The Cost of Discipleship*.

28. Puls, *Road Home*, 51.

In Greek, the word translated as "endurance" is the word *hypomeno*. *Hypomeno* is a compound word that combines the prefix *hypo*, which means "under" (as in hypodermic, "under skin"), and *meno*, which means "remain." To endure in Paul's context, then, means "to remain under" the weight of whatever suffering we are facing for the current season of time. In our culture of "quick-fix solutions," as Friedman describes us, we in the church can tend to sabotage our own spiritual growth by preventing ourselves—and those that we love—from feeling the pain related to our losses (both perceived and actual).[29] We allow our anxiety to interrupt the development of our character-in-Christ, the very essential process necessary to develop us into the empathic and forgiving people God would have us become.[30] We need to equip our organizations in how to increase our tolerance of one another's pain, while we, in love, walk with one another through the very losses that in time will produce Christlike character in us.[31] We need to let our anxiety-based entitlement die in order for us to develop an environment of interpersonal forgiveness.

Application #3: Modeling Missional Empathy

Finally, although Christians have known themselves historically to be the "people of the Book" (the Bible) and the Table (Holy Communion), we have allowed culture to define what is meant by both. Without daily growth and maintenance in the word of God, our identity in Christ can "leak out," causing us to become as self-absorbed as the society into which we have been sent as "ministers of reconciliation" (2 Cor 5:18–20). We have forgotten that we are a people who have been "sent." Therefore, our message has lost its power since it has lost its model within us. We need to regain our identity as an anamnesis community, rooted in the witness of the cross and the resurrection, and empowered by the Holy Spirit to advance the new community of Jesus along with its perfect-tense value system.

---

29. Friedman, *Failure of Nerve*, 53.

30. Friedman, *Failure of Nerve*, 69. See also Augsburger, *Caring Enough to Forgive*, 80, where he writes, "The result of empathic forgiving in community is the establishment of an empathic milieu."

31. Puls, *Road Home*, 38, writes, "We don't want to remember because we fear the resurrection of buried pain, but the pain is the portal through which we must pass in order to forgive. Remembered pain is just that: a memory, and it cannot do further harm."

As Nathan R. Frise and Mark R. McMinn posit in their article, "Forgiveness and Reconciliation: The Differing Perspectives of Psychologists and Christian Theologians," the purpose of forgiveness "is not to feel better, but to deepen and enrich community.... It is a way of life; not an inner way of life, but a way of living with others."[32] We need to teach our organizations every week a reminder of who they are in Christ as well as what we have been called to be and do as we embody an eschatological view to God's greater mosaic, the here and not-yet.

In their research article, "On Earth as It Is in Heaven: Healing through Forgiveness," Brandon J. Griffin, Caroline R. Lavelock, and Everett L. Worthington Jr. gently admonish the church with a reminder of our task: "Christ charged his followers to live according to the principles of love and forgiveness so that all people might recognize the eschatological Kingdom of God by how Christians treat one another (Matt 5:43–48; John 13:34–35). The Apostle Paul recapitulated this idea when he argued that Christians must imitate Christ in their relationships with one another in anticipation of their Lord's return (Phil 2:5–11). Even more, Paul argued, Christians possess a ministry to reconcile all people to the divine forgiveness available in Christ (2 Cor 5:18–19). It is thus a Christian's ministry of forgiveness to all humans, believers and nonbelievers, that establishes people of faith as the instruments of God's forgiving work in addition to being recipients of divine forgiveness."[33]

As previously stated, it appears that we have forgotten who we are. We, as leaders of God's larger movement, bear the responsibility for that. As leaders go, so goes the organization. Therefore, we need to equip our people with the values and practices of an anamnesis community—rooted in the perfect-tense events of the cross and resurrection, and sent to embody and ambassador love and forgiveness in a world that desperately needs it, but may not yet understand it. We need to redirect the self-centered and often narcissistic values of our overly anxious organizations toward a new missiological view of our partnership in forgiveness. We need to remind ourselves, and all whom we lead, that our lives together form a grand mosaic that is best viewed from a cross . . . and from within a "perfect(ed)" past.

Yet, within our humanness, sometimes that mosaic view makes us negotiate with our pain—a process called "bargaining." Historically, we are not alone. Check out Hannah's story.

---

32. Frise and McMinn, "Forgiveness and Reconciliation," 85.
33. Griffin et al., "On Earth," 256.

A Prophet in Time: Hannah

THE EMOTIONAL SCARS OF her broken heart ran deep as Hannah poured out her lament before Adonai. Tears, long in coming, dripped from the corners of her eyes, gently cascading down the sides of her nose and cheeks and dropping onto the chest piece of her ivory colored *simlah,* creating an expanding spot of distended grief. Elkanah had tried repeatedly to cajole his wife out of her despair, but he could not draw her out of the small bed chamber that they shared while guests at his brother's home. The room was barely lit by a single candle perched on the side table next to where Hannah sat. It provided just enough light for him to make out the tear-stained garment that enrobed the silhouette of the woman he loved more than life.

This was an annual ritual, it seemed to Elkanah, occurring each time they planned the trip to Shiloh to worship at the tabernacle there. He almost dreaded the week leading up to their journey for inevitably the tension in the home would escalate causing Hannah to isolate herself in her misery and Peninnah, Elkanah's other wife, to torment her mercilessly. Truth be told, he himself wanted to vacate the house during that week just to maintain his own sanity. True, Peninnah was his wife too, chosen in marriage because of Hannah's infertility. That was the way things were done. But Hannah was his love, his true betrothed.

Elkanah was not overt with how he differentiated his feelings—at least, he didn't think so. But his wives knew. They could see it. For example, every year at Shiloh, Elkanah would divide his returned portion of the peace offering into equal segments for Peninnah and their children, but he always gave a double amount to Hannah. Perhaps it was his way of easing the verbal torture Hannah had to endure from Peninnah (yes, he had seen its effect on her). Or perhaps it was his way of trying to compensate for the anguish he knew he could not fix. Over the years, however, Peninnah had become jealous for her husband's affections and regularly took out her jealousy on Hannah. Elkanah felt trapped in this relational dilemma, and he wasn't sure how to make it all work.

"Hannah, please," he pleaded from the doorway in whispered tones. "Don't listen to her. Peninnah didn't mean it, I'm sure. Come. Come to the table and eat. You haven't eaten anything all day. This is the offering. The *offering*! It's good! Come on, Hannah!" Then, after a pause, "Look, we leave for home tomorrow. Let's not dishonor my brother's hospitality."

Hannah said nothing in the moment. Her husband meant well, but he really didn't understand the depth of her pain, the grief that constantly poured into and out of her vacant womb. How could he understand? From her perspective, Peninnah had given children to him. So, this other woman did for her husband what she herself could not do. That made Hannah envious and bitter. It also made Peninnah self-righteous and vicious with her comments toward her rival, constantly exposing her barrenness with mean-spirited words. Every year it was the same. *Every* year.

For much of her life Hannah had dreamed about becoming a mother. She found great joy in the idea of providing children for her husband—especially sons to carry on the family name. She had watched her mother and grandmother fulfill their roles over the years, purposefully learning under their mentoring the duties that one day would be hers. Now, in marriage, she longed to live out her destiny. Yet, day after day, year after year, no matter how they tried, no matter how earnestly she prayed, she remained childless. She could see the disappointment in Elkanah's eyes, though he would never, ever say anything. It was out of barren desperation for her husband's happiness that she urged him to select another to marry so that he might have the children he longed for. When reluctantly he did so, with Peninnah, she grieved not only her ongoing loss, but also the decision that would divide his heart from hers. Her grief was deep, her anguish layered, her bitterness entrenched.

"Hannah . . ." Elkanah softened his words as he moved further into the room, closer to his wife. "Come. Let's go to the table." He reached out and took Hannah by the hand and gently, caringly pulled her up from the chair. Lovingly, he wiped the tears from her cheeks, grabbed her *mitpahat* from the chair behind where she had been siting and draped it around her shoulders, allowing the bulk of the scarf to cover the tear-spots on her *simlah*. He then kissed her forehead, held her hand, interlocking his fingers with hers, and together they went to their host's table and sat.

A Prophet in Time: Hannah

The aromas of the offering meat were rich. Elkanah's sister-in-law had embellished the table with homemade breads, vegetables, and wine. All ate heartily—all except Hannah who only picked at her food, giving the impression of eating so as not to offend her hosts. After the meal, Elkanah and Hannah returned to the bed chamber where Hannah once again sat in the lone chair in the corner of the room, tears returning to her eyes.

"Why are you weeping so?" Elkanah finally asked. "Why is your heart so sad? Is it what Peninnah had said? Don't listen to her! *Ishti*, my wife, am I not more to you than ten sons?"[1]

Despite Elkanah's affectionate tone, Hannah felt ashamed. And her shame made her bitter with grief. Now sobbing, she stood quickly, startling her husband. Covering her head with the *mitpahat* that still draped over her shoulders, she bolted from the room. Exiting her brother-in-law's house, she ran, aimlessly at first, but then on to the only place she could think of that might quiet her anguishing soul—the tabernacle, the sanctuary of Adonai.

Entering the area designated for women, Hannah moved as close to the inner court as was allowed. Falling to her knees she began to pour out her voiceless prayers to Adonai once again, mouthing her lamentations within the imposing silence of the sanctuary space, her tears punctuating each phrase of her prayer. Her hands alternated between covering her heart to emphasize her anguish and caressing her abdomen as a plea for healing. In her prayer, she made a vow before Adonai saying, "O, Jehovah Tzva'ot, Lord of the heavenly hosts, if only you will look on the misery of your servant, and remember me, and not forget your servant, but will give to your servant a male child, then I will set him before you in service to you until the day of his death."[2] She prayed repeatedly with bitter tears, her mouth forming the soundless words of her lamentation as she negotiated with the Most High.

Hannah had not noticed Eli, the high priest, sitting in his usual seat near the doorposts of the inner court, but he saw her. He saw how she staggered in and how she dropped to her knees in what looked to him to be a fit of agitation. He watched as she kept rubbing her abdomen and as her face contorted with convulsant sobs and voiceless words. He thought that she must be drunk with wine—a disgrace to bring such behavior into the sanctuary. He needed to confront her and exit her from the tabernacle before others would see her

---

1. 1 Sam 1:8.
2. 1 Sam 1:11.

condition and cause a stir that he, quite frankly, did not have the energy to deal with. Jumping up from his seat, he strode over to where Hannah knelt, his priestly garments billowing with each stride causing the bells on the hem of his blue robe to tinkle loudly with every determined step.

"How long will you make a drunken spectacle of yourself?" Eli spat his words with formal consternation. "Put away your wine! This behavior is unacceptable—especially in the sanctuary of the Most High!"[3]

Hannah was startled and immediately embarrassed by the high priest's address. Quietly, she answered him: "No, my lord, I am a woman deeply troubled; I have drunk neither wine nor strong drink, but I have been pouring out my soul before Adonai. Do not regard your servant as a worthless woman, for I have been speaking out of my great anxiety and vexation all this time."[4]

Hearing her speak so coherently and seeing the emotions by which she represented her story, Eli believed her. Moved with compassion, he said to Hannah, "Go in peace; may the Mighty One of Israel grant the petition you have made."[5]

Composing herself, Hannah replied, "Let your servant find favor in your sight." She then stood and returned to her brother-in-law's house, finally feeling that her prayer had been heard. Her deep sadness quelled, she realized that she was hungry—a sign that her season of grief had shifted. She found leftover food from the earlier meal and ate with a glad heart, leaving Elkanah wondering what had transpired to change the countenance of his wife's face.[6] Whatever it was, it encouraged him, and he joined Hannah in a second round of food.

The next morning, after worshiping once more in the sanctuary, they thanked their hosts and then traveled back to their own home. On the way, Hannah shared with Elkanah about her vow and the words of the high priest. She told him that receiving his blessing seemed to calm the aching in her soul, giving her a deep sense of peace. Elkanah listened patiently, taking Hannah's hand and caressing it with affection, unsure of whether to open his heart to hope for his wife.

In due time, Elkanah and Hannah were intimate, and by Adonai's grace, she became pregnant. For nine months, she glowed with an inner

3 1 Sam 1:14.
4. 1 Sam 1:15–16.
5. 1 Sam 1:17.
6. 1 Sam 1:18.

joy, knowing in her heart that Adonai had answered her prayer. As her son made his entrance into the world, Hannah heard the words of her vow echoing within her memory. She knew that one day—a day that would come all too quickly—she would need to fulfill her promise. But in this moment, as she gazed into the face of the child—her son—her joy was matchless.

"You have a son!" she exclaimed to Elkanah, through tears, as she was recovering from the excruciating pains of delivery. "Adonai gave us *a son*!" The news of that moment bonded husband and wife, redeeming years of anguish, and causing the pangs of labor to dissipate quickly.

"A boy!" Elkanah declared to the room. "*Ishti*, what shall we name him? Shall we use my father's name—Jeroham? Or your father's?"

"Samuel," Hannah replied to her husband's exuberance. "Let's name him Samuel—'God has heard'—since I have asked him of Adonai.[7] Is that okay?"

"Samuel." Elkanah said the name aloud to gauge its effect, as he gazed at his son's pouting face. "Yes, Samuel. Samuel it is!"

They continued to rejoice together at the miraculous nature of this birth, marveling at what Adonai had done for them.

What Adonai was truly birthing in that moment, however, was yet to be revealed. A prophetic glimpse of that plan came pouring out of the Hannah as she, anointed by the Spirit, lifted up words of praise:

> My heart exults in Adonai!
> My dignity has been restored by Adonai!
> I can gloat over my enemies,
> because of my joy at your saving me.
> No one is as holy as Adonai,
> because there is none to compare with you,
> no rock like our God.
> Stop your proud boasting!
> Don't let arrogance come from your mouth!
> For Adonai is a God of knowledge,
> and he appraises actions.
> The bows of the mighty are broken,
> while the feeble are armed with strength.
> The well-fed hire themselves for bread,
> while those who were hungry hunger no more.
> The barren woman has borne seven,
> while the mother of many wastes away.
> Adonai kills and makes alive;
> he brings down to the grave, and he brings up.

---

7. 1 Sam 1:20.

> Adonai makes poor, and he makes rich;
> he humbles, and he exalts.
> He raises the poor from the dust,
> lifts up the needy from the trash pile;
> he gives them a place with leaders
> and assigns them seats of honor.
> For the earth's pillars belong to Adonai;
> on them he has placed the world.
> He will guard the steps of his faithful,
> but the wicked will be silenced in darkness.
> For it is not by strength that a person prevails—
> those who fight Adonai will be shattered;
> he will thunder against them in heaven—
> Adonai will judge the ends of the earth.
> He will strengthen his king
> and enhance the power of his anointed.[8]

Hannah's words flowed freely, as if they came from a source external to herself. A large portion of what she said surprised both her and Elkanah. Yet, these words would be remembered over the period of Samuel's weaning, giving courage to Hannah, and reminding her that Adonai redeems all things, most especially when the time came for her to bring the child to the high priest in fulfillment of her bargain. Their annual visits to the tabernacle gave both Hannah and Elkanah the opportunity to watch their baby boy become a young man of incredible wisdom and stature. They marveled at how Adonai was transforming the life of their son—a life that once had been born out of desperation and grief.

Only many years later would history reveal to them just how important that foundation of desperation and grief would be for both the glorious and devastating days yet to come for Adonai's children.

As Samuel grew up, Adonai was with him and blessed every word that came out of his mouth. And all Israel from Dan to Beersheba knew that Samuel was a trustworthy prophet of Adonai. The Mighty One continued to appear at Shiloh, for Adonai revealed himself to Samuel at Shiloh in divine wisdom and the prophetic word.[9]

And with each prophetic word uttered, Hannah smiled, and thanked the One Who Provided.

---

8. 1 Sam 2:1–10 CJB.
9. 1 Sam 3:19–21.

3

Bargaining

Grief is a transitional process, not a transactional one.

But Hannah answered, "No, my lord, I am a woman deeply troubled; I have drunk neither wine nor strong drink, but I have been pouring out my soul before the Lord. Do not regard your servant as a worthless woman, for I have been speaking out of my great anxiety and vexation all this time."

—1 Samuel 1:15–16

I love to bargain. I inherited that quality from my dad. Buying a car, buying a house—the process of negotiating a good deal stimulates the creative and competitive sides of my personality. I do my research. I anticipate what the appropriate "wiggle room" might require. I think through what the seller's needs might be. Then, I come up with a game plan. The plan is fair, of course, but my objective is to create a pathway that gets me a better deal than the original asking price. The entire process is fun for me. Getting into the mind of the seller, anticipating their next move, devising counter offers—it's what makes bargaining exciting.

    Except when it's not. Bargaining within the difficult situations of death and loss is not fun. Not at all. In fact, I hate it. I hate being put into what feels like a no-win scenario.

The problem is, I don't often get to choose those scenarios. They choose me. Some of them come at me because of the intrinsic unfairness or rhythms of life. Some, due to the unfortunate choices that I have made for myself or within the arenas of my leadership. Some, because of the really good decisions that I have made, but for which I have to face into the ramifications of those decisions. Certainly, some endings can be good—even "necessary," as Henry Cloud argues in *Necessary Endings: The Employees, Businesses, and Relationships that All of Us Have to Give Up in Order to Move Forward*, clearly what I consider to be one of the best leadership books of all time.[1] Some endings, however, can be quite debilitating.

"Death" in any form can suck the life out of a leader. Certainly, the death of loved ones does—a spouse, a parent, a close friend, a child. (Especially a child. The death of a child is brutal. Any of these significant losses can be devastating, for sure. But the loss of your child? It forever changes you. You "move on," of course, because you have to, because society tells you to, because you need to pay your bills. But a part of you dies when your child dies.) In fact, just the *anticipation* of any of these pending personal losses is enough to derail a leader's capacity to make decisions, organize their own thoughts, stay focused on their work objectives, and to be fully present in any meeting of any kind. Having to negotiate their own emotions, let alone the emotions of others around them, can create a unique vortex for a leader that sucks them into an out-of-control whirlwind of anxiety and obfuscated loyalties.

Yet, "death" can happen in other ways, too. What about these examples:

- When a leader's vision for their organization dies
- When an organization has grown beyond the leader's capacity, and everyone knows it but the leader
- The death of a leader's reputation—caused perhaps by the violation of ethical boundaries
- The expansion of a leader's reputation—causing a forced change to their family's privacy and preferred schedule
- The death of a friendship—caused by a promotion where the friend is now your boss, or you are theirs
- A friend betrays you, compromising your reputation and your job

---

1. Cloud, *Necessary Endings*.

- The death of a marriage that occurs because your obsessive need to prove yourself keeps you at work all hours of the day and night rather than with your family
- The ending of a role that you've had—because your child has now left home, or has gotten married
- The death of your freedom when that child moves back home
- The death of your sanity when that child decides to marry the spawn of Satan
- The ending brought about by being transferred to another job, church, or city
- The death of your vitality that comes from being falsely accused of sexual misconduct
- The death of an ability brought on by age-related or injury-related physical limitations or dysfunctions
- The shifting of loyalties due to a promotion
- The daily deaths experienced in team morale because your leadership role now requires you to fire someone that you care about

Most leaders have had to make critical decisions, fire people, reposition roles, set limits on the behaviors of their employees, or defend themselves against character assassination attempts. And most leaders have had to face into the painful processes of negotiating with their own emotions regarding those decisions. Some leaders have had to develop a thick skin to buffer those difficult emotions. Other leaders, like me, have had to learn how to balance the equally important values of mercy and leadership—so that one value does not supplant the other, threatening to sabotage either the mission of the organization or the relationships that are important to them.

A LAND OF MILK AND HONEY?

Let's face it. Every change inspired or experienced by a leader, both positive and negative, comes with a price tag—loss. Change, as a rule, asks people to leave the comforts of their status quo and to travel to an unknown reality that promises to be a proverbial "land flowing with milk and honey" (Exod 3:8), with "plans for [our] welfare and not for harm" (Jer 29:11). In other words, we leaders propose changes that are supposed to make life better—for our constituents and, hopefully, ourselves. At least, ideally, that's the plan.

To get to that promised land, however, we must leave "home," just as Abram initially was called to do (Gen 12:1–4). Leaders, by definition, are called to lead others to greater fruit-bearing and productivity. Therefore, by nature of their role, they become purveyors of loss and grief—change. Yet not every leader knows how to negotiate with the emotions of loss and grief sufficiently to assist their followers, their organizations, in moving confidently into that new reality.

As I stated earlier, grief is our normal human reaction to change. The more intense the change, the more intense the grief response will be. As a "stage" in that grief process, bargaining is one of the coping strategies we use to come to terms with a loss that is too great for us to bear on our own.

BARGAINING: WRESTLING WITH LOSS

Simply put, bargaining is how we *negotiate with the pain of our loss*[2]—regardless as to whether that loss is perceived, anticipated, or transpired. Whether it is personal or corporate, loss can make us feel numb, directionless, confused (emotionally, mentally, spiritually), paralyzed by fear, helpless, hopeless, vulnerable, out of control. Bargaining is a coping mechanism that we use to try to regain some sense of balance to a perceived out-of-balance situation. As we bargain within the grief process, we appeal to someone or something that we perceive to be more "powerful" or who might have what we want or need, and *we leverage ourselves as an interventional strategy*. In other words, we stand in the gap of the projected loss, and we try to negotiate for a better deal, a better outcome—an outcome that benefits us and/or the people that we care about.

And we're not alone. People of faith have been doing that for a very long time.

When faced with the prospects of judgment on the city of Sodom, Abraham negotiated several times with the theophanic envoy, utilizing a litany of conditional clauses—"but what if only fifty ... forty-five ... forty ... thirty ... twenty ... ten righteous people left in Sodom ... what about then? Would you still destroy the city?" (Gen 18:23–33). For the astute reader of the story, we know that Abraham's relative Lot was in Sodom,

---

2. Adapted from Kübler-Ross and Kessler, *On Grief and Grieving*, 17.

along with his family. So, Abraham leveraged his influence with God on behalf of his relatives.

Challenged with the ramifications of his divine call (as well as the need to confront his fate with his brother, Esau), Jacob "wrestled" with God's angelic heavyweight, negotiating a blessing to accompany his displaced hip and rechristened name (Gen 32:24–31). I can imagine that conversation, can't you? I've had similar "wrestling matches" with God—especially following my heart attack (see the introduction) as the Lord began to lay out a path for me that was much more difficult than I had ever expected. One of the best lines in the entire Bible, in my opinion, is Gen 32:31: "The sun rose upon him as he passed Penuel, *limping because of his hip*" (italics mine). When we bargain with God, we are forever changed—and often we have the scars to prove it.

Then there's the incredibly difficult story of Jephthah in Judg 11. Previously rejected and evicted by his relatives because of his parentage (i.e., his mother was a prostitute), his outlier marauding skills eventually place him in leadership over Israel during a time of enemy attacks. His judgmental ousters now need his street-learned guerilla warfare tactics to save them. In what looks like a moment of arrogant machismo, Jephthah makes a vow before God that if God grants him victory over his opponent, then "whoever comes out of the doors of my house to meet me, when I return victorious from the Ammonites, shall be the Lord's, to be offered up by me as a burnt offering" (Judg 11:31). You know the story. It is Jephthah's daughter, his only child, that is the first to come out of his house upon his return. It is she who must become Jephthah's burnt offering sacrifice to the Lord (Judg 11:39) in fulfillment of his vow.

Bargaining, I contend, is in the proverbial job description of any prophetic leader. By the nature of their call, genuine prophets—both ancient and modern—bargain on behalf of the people they care about. I would argue that it's in their DNA whether they acknowledge it or not. Even a cursory reading of the Hebrew scriptures will catalogue prophets negotiating with God on behalf of God's people in either overt or subtle ways. Amos, Habakkuk, Ezekiel, Nahum, Jeremiah, Isaiah, even Jonah—they plead with God for God's redemptive intervention, for the shifting of God's judgments, for God's forgiveness of God's recalcitrant people, for the execution of God's vengeance on the enemies of God's children. Yet, not all these chosen messengers would qualify as stand-up citizens in God's heavenly domain. They are fully human. They have their own stories, their own personalities, their own strengths of character, and their own flaws. They are just like us.

According to God's infinite, often mind-boggling wisdom, God uniquely calls individuals with various personalities, backgrounds, hang-ups, abilities, levels of maturity, and perspectives, and places them into contexts within which they must be messengers of both divine judgment and missional re-alignment. In fact, it seems God calls specific individuals to be prophets *because* God knows they will plead passionately on behalf of God's people, regardless of how angry or disappointed those people make God feel, much like a defense attorney would in a court of law.

I wonder. In situations of loss, both perceived and actual, do we modern day prophets plead with God on behalf of the people we are called to care for, for the people of the churches and organizations that we lead? And does anyone plead with God on our behalf—that our losses may find residence in the embrace of those who care for us?

Within difficult scenarios, prophet-leaders tend to negotiate while on the battlefield of pain. It is when we're facing into our losses that we may make promises—to God, to "someone in control" when we're feeling out of control, or even to ourselves. And we implicate ourselves within that promise. Typically, we barter by using *our* current or future behavior, status, attitudes, faith choices, or relationships as a bargaining chip. "Lord, if you heal my son, then I will never miss a Sunday worship service . . . quit drinking . . . give more money to the poor . . . serve you for the rest of my life . . ." "Lord, if you help our company get out of debt, I promise to rebrand with a cross at the center of our logo." "God, if you convince my wife not to leave me, I'll never, ever have another affair."

Sound familiar? I dare say, we've all done some bargaining when faced with the potential for loss. Have you ever negotiated with God and made a promise that governed the rest of your life?

JANE'S PROMISE

In one of the churches that I previously served, one of my leaders was Jane (not her real name). Jane was a formidable woman in that congregation. By the time I met her she was in her seventies and widowed. Her children were grown and out of the house, so she lived alone. She was one of the people in charge of the church kitchen and often had to be appeased if events were requiring the use of the kitchen and its contents. Because of her often-reactionary personality and long-tenured influence in the congregation, people generally accommodated Jane. Truthfully, many were simply intimated by her.

In addition to Jane's "rough" exterior, however, was a heart that loved serving the poor and the marginalized. In many ways, that's how she worshiped God. On a regular basis, she would go to the community grocery stores and broker deals with the managers, obtaining donations of day-old or date-sensitive food items and bring them to the church's food bank. She would also create monthly meals at the church for seniors within the community, giving them not only food, but also opportunities for fellowship. And she provided many years' worth of funeral luncheons—hot meals—to assist families that were grieving, quite often absorbing the costs herself when the family could not pay. By reputation, she had served in these capacities for nearly six decades—until her health took a turn for the worse, requiring her to step down from her roles.

During the months prior to Jane's death, I had one of my rare heart-to-heart conversations with her. I reflected on her many years of service and thanked her for all that she had done for the church and community over the years. I then asked her why she had devoted so much of her life to serving in this way. I'll never forget her response.

"When I was young," she said, "my husband and I just couldn't have children. We tried and tried, but I never got pregnant. So, I prayed to God. I told God that if he gave me a child, I would serve him in the church the rest of my life. And God answered my prayer, so that's why I did what I did. I served by doing what I knew how to do. And if I didn't know how to do something, I figured it out."

It was Hannah's story mentoring yet another generation.

Jane's lifetime of service was certainly not all "puppies and sunshine," to quote Paul Miller, my good friend and colleague. For sure, there were times when Jane and I clashed over significant issues. Jane demanded a lot from her pastors. Much of what she demanded was rooted in her anxiety that she would not be able to carry out her vow to God. Yet on the day of her funeral, we honored her life of service, a decades old story of faithfulness to her word. Jane got what she bargained for. And dare I say, so did God.

And so did Hannah.

HANNAH, THE PROPHET?

It would seem natural to identify Hannah as a prophet based mostly on her prophetic "song" recorded in 1 Sam 2:1–10, since it portrays the challenges besetting the people of Israel in the years to come, as well as God's intentions for her son within them. However, I contend that Hannah is a prophet not so much because of what she said, but by how God embodied within her barrenness and subsequent pregnancy a unique glimpse at God's character, as well as God's mosaic plan and purpose. Certainly, she gives birth to Samuel, and Samuel is recorded to have been a significant prophet and leader over Israel. But I would argue that it was Hannah that "lived" the prophetic message of the divine plan, as well as God's unique interventional strategy to rescue God's people from their rebellious ways, years before Samuel took on his prophetic call. As such, she joins an impressive line of miraculous, prophetic baby-makers.

Hannah's story is one that we had seen before with Sarah (and Abraham) in Gen 15–21, and will see again with Manoah's wife (Samson's mother) in Judg 13, as well as with Elizabeth (and Zechariah) in Luke 1—childless couples, frustrated and beyond hope for seeing the blessing of offspring, encounter a God who acts within impossible circumstances to remind Israel (and all of us) of God's grander plan. Repeatedly within the scriptural metanarrative we read that "for mortals it is impossible, but for God all things are possible" (Matt 19:26). God is not limited by our limitations. Ultimately, that was demonstrated by yet another miraculous birth within yet another impossible scenario—Jesus, the child born as a divine interventional strategy by supernatural means with the consent of a single teenage girl who had no possible reason to be found pregnant at the time (Luke 1–2).

This story line of supernatural births graphically depicts a prophetic message of hope given by God to God's people exactly when their need for deliverance is most profoundly felt (at least by some), their recalcitrance is exceptionally obstinate, and their blindness to God's mosaic plan has kept them disconnected from their calling to be a light to the world. Each of these birth stories pivots the trajectory of God's interventional plan, realigning yet again the people of faith to consider their call while God's divine mission plows forward regardless of their response.

Hannah, like her biblical sister-midwives, acts in her own way as a *theotokos*, a "God-bearer," bringing to birth a message of hope—not just by giving her people a model of lamentable prayer for times of barrenness and want, nor by virtue of her ability to sing prophetically about God's redemptive story to be played out by her newborn baby, nor by her giving birth to Samuel, one of the most historically significant prophetic, priestly, and even military influencers within the Hebrew Scriptures. Now, I realize that I'm using a term that historically references Mary, the mother of Jesus, especially within the theological frame of Eastern Christianity. Yet, I would argue that Hannah and her biblical colleagues are "types" of *theotokoi* (the plural of *theotokos*) because what was carried and birthed by each of them into the world was, prophetically, a physical manifestation of the divine incarnational initiative—a reminder that God remains faithful to God's promises even when conditions seem impossible, even when our own integrity is in question.[3]

I would argue that Hannah's barrenness prophetically represents Israel's (and by proxy, humanity's) fruitless life apart from the life-giving grace of God—an embodiment of divine grief and disappointment at how Israel consistently rebelled against God, exerted independence from their covenantal relationship, and incessantly pursued other gods for their provisions, rather than drawing in repentance and faith to Adonai, their first love. Hannah's miracle birth story prophesies that God's divine mission moves forward through those who come in repentance, willing to sacrifice everything important to them for the sake of being captured by God's grace. Hannah, Sarah, Manoah's wife, Elizabeth, and Mary . . . might even be considered real-time human examples of what Jesus would one day teach about in the parable of the hidden treasure (Matt 13:44), or the pearl of great price (Matt 13:45–46), or the parable of the lost coin (Luke 15:8–10). The divine initiative is at hand. Jesus makes that point in the Upper Room Discourse of John's Gospel: "Abide in me as I abide in you. Just as the branch cannot bear fruit by itself unless it abides in the vine, neither can you unless you abide in me. I am the vine, you are the branches. Those who abide in me and I in them bear much fruit, because apart from me you can do nothing" (15:4–5). God responds to those whose hearts are primed and ready to be vessels for God's interventional strategy.

I would also argue that Hannah's prophetic life story introduces a vitally important category to our understanding of personal and corporate loss—a category that I have called *congenital grief*, a legacy of grief into which a person, group, or organization is born.[4] As prophet-leaders, we deal with congenital grief all the time. Let me explain.

---

3. For an excellent post-modern exploration of *theotokos*, see Dean and Foster, *God-bearing Life*.

4. In more recent years, studies in trauma have offered newer names for this

CONGENITAL GRIEF

"My life began in the midst of tremendous sorrow and grief and, like Frodo's near mortal wound from a Morgul-blade at the foot of Weathertop, mine was a wound that has never completely healed. Ultimately, its eternal purposes, fully known only to God, yielded a hunger to know the one who lived, died, and lived again. And for that I am eternally grateful."[5]

So begins the memoir of Michael Christian Shaw, pastor, singer/songwriter, award winning artist, and one of my dearest friends. His newly published book, *Faithful Are the Wounds: A Memoir*, tells the story of how the tragic death of his four-and-a-half-year-old brother, Brucie, dying when Mike was only nine days old, infiltrated every facet of his life and ministry through the influence of his parents' overwhelming grief and deeply embedded traumatic pain. Mike was nurtured into the grief of his parents' loss early on—a grief that would form a perfect-tense shadow that would follow him into life and affect every major decision and event in the years to come. *Faithful Are the Wounds*, however, demonstrates how such unresolved generational grief can precipitate God's redemptive healing, prophetically inviting us to see a larger mosaic design to God's unfolding drama of our distinctly human story.

As with the prophet Samuel's birth, Mike's story illustrates what I refer to as *congenital grief*—a grief into which a person, a family, a group, a church, or an organization is born, and out of which flows conscious or unconscious influences that impact how we live, both individually as well as within community with others. For example, congenital grief may occur after the following:

- A couple chooses to get pregnant soon after a miscarriage, or the death of a significant loved one, or prior to one of them being deployed in the military, or within or following a traumatic event

- A church experiences a merger, and the "new" congregation must reorient itself apart from the way things were done in the past

---

phenomena—"transgenerational grief," or "epigenetics," for example. See Moeller, "Transgenerational Grief"; Segal, "When the Grief"; or Kathleen Curzie Gajdos, "Intergenerational Effects." While the principle is the same—that unresolved grief has the capacity to reproduce itself into subsequent generations—I'm using my term "congenital grief" within my context here to illustrate the reproducibility narrative that grief can have on the life of a leader and an organization.

5. Shaw, *Faithful Are the Wounds*, ix.

- A new pastor is hired following the termination of the former pastor due to sexual boundary violations, and the congregation's leaders exert more accountability expectations on the new pastor to prevent future violations
- A company acquires a competitor organization and decides to keep all of the employees of that acquired company, yet expecting those employees to conform to the new business culture
- A congregation hires a new youth pastor and reboots the student ministry after the suicide of the previous youth pastor
- A church splits due to a conflict and those who exit form a new congregation
- A new leader is not trusted by the organization because she happens to be related to the former CEO who was convicted of embezzlement

Regardless of the context, congenital grief exhibits specific characteristics, especially relevant within the bargaining stage of grief.

Congenital Grief Is Not Rooted in a Current Loss

Congenital grief engages real-time participants into emotional triangles with past participants' pain. The originating loss has occurred prior to the present time, illustrating a perfect-tense grief expression—a single event in the past but the impact of which continues into the present, as previously described in chapter 2. My friend Mike lived his life under the emotional weight of his parents' grief. Their unresolved grief emotions unintentionally were passed on to Mike. Mike became triangled by a traumatic pain that was not his own. Rather, he inherited it—a legacy that was bequeathed to him by his parents through their estate of pain. This triangulating occurs in marriages, families, groups, churches, and organizations all the time. The prophet-leader needs to realize that anytime we negotiate with pain—our own or on behalf of those we care about—there is the potential that such pain has a perfect-tense history that predates the current situation.

Congenital Grief Often Reveals Itself in Seasons of Conflict

Historical losses are stowed away in our memories. Unless we are intentional about doing so, they are rarely talked about—at times, even becoming taboo topics, based on the level of trauma, shame, or avoidance that they represent. Yet because they often contain unresolved emotions that still hold sway over us within our current contexts, they will reveal themselves in times of anxiety or relational tension—especially during conflicts. Conflicts, by nature, stir up embedded emotional triangles.[6] In the heat of the moment, those triangles will implicate people, events, or memories that are present-day reflections of unresolved past emotions. Prophet-leaders are uniquely called to gently expose the hidden family secrets and long-tenured unspoken rules that lurk under the carpets of our organizations, preventing genuine productivity and growth. To the willing mosaic-minded observer, symptoms of such triangles will reveal themselves—repeated unexplainable angry outbursts, recurrent patterns of boundary violations (like affairs or sexual misconduct), chronic situations involving alcohol abuse, pornography, illicit drugs, or the misuse of prescription medicine, chronic depression in the leader or the organization not otherwise diagnosed as organic in nature (a topic so important that I deal with it in chapter five), overcompensation and workaholism, abuse of power, expressions of apathy or boredom in the leader, or recurrent self-sabotage, to name a few.

Congenital Grief Reminds Us that Losses Accumulate[7]

We don't live in a vacuum. Every decision that we make that negatively impacts ourselves or someone else, every action and reaction that causes someone else to stumble or us to fail in character, every broken relationship, every firing of an employee, every foul word uttered at us in contempt for our leadership . . . they store up within a compendium of accumulated losses. If those losses remain unprocessed, over time they leak out into other areas of our lives. They may even accrue into a "statement of retained earnings" that negatively impacts our most significant "shareholders"—our children, our marriages, our partnerships, our churches, our organizations. They don't necessarily show up in a corporate annual report, but they most definitely affect our annualized rate of return. These losses form equities within the family, church, or organization that inevitably bequeath ownership of unresolved grief to the next generation. Facing into accumulated losses requires the prophet-leader to develop a long-term investment strategy for assisting

---

6. See Woolverton, *Mission Rift*, for more on this topic.

7. For an incredibly compassionate discussion on this theme, see Jeffreys, *Helping Grieving People*.

those involved in seeing the redemptive value of grief within God's larger mosaic plan. I'll explore how to do that later in this chapter.

Congenital Grief Tells a Family Story, a History—Reminding Us that Each of Us Is Connected Within Community

For sure, whether congenital or not, grief is individually processed—meaning that not everyone grieves in the same way, with the same expressions, or within the same timelines. In other words, just because someone "didn't cry at the funeral," doesn't mean that they haven't cried, are in denial, or didn't love the person who died. It might just mean that we haven't seen *how* that person grieves.

Also, how someone grieves is often learned from within their family of nurture. I say "family of nurture" instead of "family of origin" because not all of us were raised within our family of origin. Some of us were adopted. Some were raised within the foster care system. Some grew up within the homes of grandparents, aunts and uncles, or caring neighbors. Within those nurturing communities, we learned—through direct experiences and observations—how to deal with the emotions of grief (or how not to deal with them, as the case may be).

We also may have learned to grieve from our ethnic and cultural background. While working as a chaplain at a West Philadelphia emergency department, a community rich in ethnic diversity, I often observed within families a wide variety of grief expressions—both overt and subtle—that were consistent with specific cultural practices related to death and loss (e.g., rituals performed, whether crying was allowed, vocalizing of lament). Most certainly, each person within those families grieved, but how they grieved was often distinct. These families taught me a lot about the need to be culturally sensitive and compassionate within each person's or family's diverse expressions of grief and loss and how to appreciate the various ways people respond to grief within their culture and customs.[8]

Additionally, grief appears to be influenced by how our prior experiences of loss have been processed. How we deal with current emotions of grief is often a reflection of how prior experiences of loss were reinforced positively or negatively (e.g., "boys don't cry," "don't be a baby," "of course it's okay to miss grandma," "why not take the time you need to say goodbye"). Prophet-leaders need to approach grief—their own as well

---

8. For more on this, see Jeffreys, *Helping Grieving People*, 21.

as other's—as formative expressions of a history that predates the present experience of loss.

Certainly, all these characteristics may apply to any type of grief, but collectively, they remind us that all our losses are part of a constellation of experiences within God's grander mosaic, each with layers of emotions that define who we are.

In the biblical story, my heart goes out to Hannah's child, Samuel. He was born into a family dynamic where his mother was already planning on giving him away once he was weaned. That has to do a number on a child's psyche, right? Then, they all had to live with the subsequent anticipatory anxiety related to that fateful day when Samuel would be disassociated from his family. Just when he establishes some sense of familial attachment with his mother, she hands him over to the high priest, establishing only annual visitation rights to bring him fresh underwear and new age-appropriate toys. By our twenty-first-century standards, this relational dynamic sadly might be approaching "normal," but it is far from being illustrative of healthy attachment theory.[9]

Samuel is born into grief—the grief of his mother's years of barrenness, the grief from the loss of familial trust and attachment, and the anticipatory grief of the role he will play within the congregation of Israel's judgment, something he begins to realize only after God calls him into his prophetic ministry (1 Sam 3). Samuel would have to learn to differentiate himself from his mother's anxiety to become fully embraced by his call to lead God's people through their season of transition—a season that would inaugurate a new chapter for the people of Israel, one that would involve being led by a king, rather than by God's prophetic envoys. And yet, by his birth narrative, Samuel would be equipped to understand God's plea to a barren Israel to return to a self-giving, ultimately incarnational God. Within God's redemptive plan, Samuel was born for such a time as this.

But did he get what his mother bargained for?

ANXIETY: THE ROOT OF BARGAINING

There are some who would call the bargaining stage of grief a "false hope" stage, an attempt at avoiding the reality of the loss.[10] Actually, I believe it

---

9. For more on attachment theory, check out Johnson, *Attachment Theory in Practice*, and Johnson, *Emotionally Focused Couple Therapy*.

10. Gault, "Five Stages of Grief," *Bargaining*, para. 2.

to be the opposite. I contend that, whenever it occurs, and regardless of its frequency of occurrence within the mosaic of our grief process, bargaining assists us in becoming grounded within the reality of our situation by gradually helping us face our anxieties related to the loss. By turning toward our pain, we are creating a mental pathway for healing—helping our mind and heart search for solid ground, something, *anything*, upon which we might stand when everything seems out of our control, and loss is inevitable.

I would argue that at the root of bargaining is anxiety—that feeling of being unsettled, unsafe, or insecure when facing a situation that moves us beyond our comfort zone, beyond our pain tolerance, beyond what is central and essential to our experience. When we feel out of control, we negotiate with our pain, and to do so, we use what we have—ourselves—as best we can as we seek grace, comfort, or the upper hand, hopefully producing a reduction to our anxiety and a return to the solid ground we long for.

Bargaining is a coping mechanism. Therefore, I also see it as a *"hoping mechanism"*—an essential part of the process of discovering, or restoring, hope within what perhaps has felt like a hopeless situation. Bargaining is not about bartering for false hope. It's about negotiating with our pain as we search for a way to redefine our reality and find meaning and purpose within our loss.[11]

And that's one of the most significant jobs of a prophet whether in the home, in the church, or in the organizations where we serve: standing in the gap of loss, and redefining hope for God's people.

Indeed, one of the most challenging things about bargaining is that it makes our loss "real." While most certainly we can go in and out of denial at various times and at various levels within our grief, the negotiation processes of bargaining serve to bring the pain of our loss to the forefront of our experience, helping us to emerge out of the layers of denial and into the redefining of our new reality. Inevitably, it's a reality we must face into, and so, we seek to strike a deal with the "one" who we perceive has the power to do what we feel powerless to do.

So, how do we do that—typically?

THE "IF-THEN" CLAUSE

Bargaining is a very normal human behavior. Many of us have an innate desire to barter—to get a better deal, a lower price, a greater product or

---

11. Kübler-Ross and Kessler, *On Grief and Grieving*, 17–19.

experience: "Is this your best offer?" "I'll give you ten dollars for the lot, instead of the twenty dollars you're asking for." "It's my anniversary—can you comp me an upgrade?"

In grief, bargaining is also normal, and it's perfectly okay to fail at it. While normal, it often illustrates how we tend to make our experiences of grief *transactional* rather than *transitional*—bartering a quid pro quo rather than moving from an experience of ending, through a period of anxiety, to a new reality that has yet to be defined.

And we do so most often with what is known as the *if–then clause*.

The if–then clause is something that most of us learned as kids in language arts class as part of the structure of conditional sentences. Conditional sentences "present situations and their possible outcomes."[12] For example, "if I throw the eraser in class, then I will get detention." While an explanation of the different types of conditional sentences is beyond the scope of this book, let me just say that, within the bargaining stage, the if–then formulary functions as one of the primary tools we use as we strive to negotiate with the pain of our loss. Therefore, it's important to note a few things about this particular tool.

- While the if–then can be quite overt ("If you rescind my termination, I promise I won't embezzle ever again"), many times it is quite subtle, and even unvoiced. For example, I may not say it aloud at all, but I may just start working ten extra hours per week to "compensate" for what I am hoping will be a "release from the punishment due to good behavior."

- It is possible to collude with others within our if–then bargaining: "Lord, if you completely heal Jason's tumor, our entire congregation will start a new ministry for cancer survivors."

- Our if–then clauses say more about us than about our pending loss. These clauses reflect our pain, our anxiety, our discomfort, our avoidance, our hopes, our needs, our vulnerability. "Ethel has come into work considerably late every day for the past two weeks without calling to let me know. If I handle some of her reports, maybe I won't have to fire her. After all, she's my friend."

---

12. Enago Academy, "If-Then," para. 1.

While the if-then clause is one of the primary tools for bargaining, there are also some specific rules for bargaining within the grief process that may help the prophet-leader make negotiating with losses more "successful."

SIX RULES FOR SUCCESSFULLY NEGOTIATING WITH YOUR LOSS

In the corporate world, there are basic rules to negotiating that, when followed, assist in bargaining successfully. I believe that there are rules that assist followers of Jesus in "successfully" negotiating with our losses, as well. I've adapted a few of those corporate rules and created a few more rules of my own to guide pastor-leaders within this bargaining stage of grief. Abiding by these rules will also equip us in helping our organizations move positively through grief as we navigate through the changes and pursue our mission.

Rule #1: Grief is a Transitional Process, Not a Transactional One

It is critically important that we not see loss as a win-lose scenario, even though it feels that way. In win-lose scenarios, our bargaining assumes a power dynamic that is adversarial. In business, that may be essential as companies vie for limited resources, brand loyalty, expansion possibilities, or basic survival of the fittest. But for followers of Jesus within the arenas of grief and loss, we must assume a more open and amenable, nonadversarial relationship. If we truly believe that God loves us, that God wants the best for us, then despite what we're feeling in any given moment, we must trust that God is going to be true to God's character, that God is going to care for us within our time of need (Ps 46:1–3 and Matt 11:28–30, for example).

Adversarial negotiations require transactions of deeds, resources, and emotions. We compromise, we give to get, we operate within quid pro quo dynamics. However, within our grief scenarios, we navigate through our bargaining with the assumption—and faith—that God cares for us, that God loves us, that God understands our losses. As such, our bargaining is *transitional* rather than transactional—leading us through a process of endings, neutral zones, and new beginnings, as William Bridges's *Managing Transitions* teaches us, assisting us in coping with the realities of our loss.

The prophet Isaiah speaks words that historically have been framed by the church as referring to Jesus, the Suffering Servant who was acquainted with our grief:

> He was despised and rejected by others; a man of suffering and acquainted with infirmity; and as one from whom others hide their faces he was despised, and we held him of no account. Surely, he has borne our infirmities and carried our diseases; yet we accounted him stricken, struck down by God, and afflicted. But he was wounded for our transgressions, crushed for our iniquities; upon him was the punishment that made us whole, and by his bruises we are healed (Isa 53:3–5).

Grief is a transitional process that moves us toward trust, and that movement is mediated through bargaining—negotiating with our pain, and, when necessary, even pleading with God on behalf of God's people.

Rule #2: Grief is a Collaborative Conversation, Not an Imposed Penal Sentence

The book of Job within the Hebrew Scriptures illustrates, among other things, that we can converse with the Almighty within the painful realities of our losses. Notice that while responding to Job's questions by pointing out his very limited view of God's grander mosaic, God never tells Job to "sit down and shut up." Certainly, we may not understand the nature of the "negotiating" that goes on between God and Satan when it comes to Job's welfare, making one wonder if humanity is but a pawn in some cosmic drama, but at no point is Job prevented from having access to the ears of the Almighty. God's response to Job's questions gives Job (and us) a brief glimpse of the divine mosaic—and the fact that humanity's questions, as raw and as real as they may be to us, are quite limited when compared to that greater design. Yet, God's immeasurable grace allows us to question, allows us to doubt, allows us to be angry, allows us to talk with the Creator of the universe openly and intimately. We do well to be honest and vulnerable with our heartfelt pleas.

Rule #3: We Need to Know the Objectives of the Other Side[13]

Astute negotiators understand that "the more you know about the other side's interests, restrictions, boundaries, and motivations, the better you'll fare in the negotiation."[14] That's fine for business deals, but grief is not a

13. Solomon, "10 Rules," para. 3.
14. Solomon, "10 Rules," para. 3.

transaction, as stated above. We may never know the "objectives" of God when it comes to the suicide death of our teenage child, or the traumatic death of a neighbor in a house fire, or the bankruptcy and closure of a town's main place of employment for thousands of workers. But, by faith, we can choose to acknowledge that God does have a larger mosaic plan, even if right now we can't see it: "For now we see in a mirror, dimly, but then we will see face to face. Now I know only in part; then I will know fully, even as I have been fully known" (1 Cor 13:12).

Having an appreciation of the biblical metanarrative in advance of any acute experiences of loss can help us negotiate more honestly: "God, every fiber of my being wants to fix this situation, but I can't. And I don't like that I can't. I would offer my life if it would turn back time and prevent what happened. I feel so frustrated and incredibly sad right now. I feel helpless and I'm hurting. I'm choosing to believe that one day you'll help me see beyond this moment, but right now, I can't. Help me, please." The role of the prophet-leader is to help translate that metanarrative into God's compassionate presence here and now, within the grief of God's children.

Rule #4: We Need to "Be on the Side" of the People We Serve[15]

Business negotiators often appeal to their opponent by acknowledging the mutual benefit of a successfully brokered deal. Doing so enables each side to "look good" to the larger community. In both personal as well as corporate losses, however, prophet-leaders give voice to *God's* greater purpose, keeping all participants aligned with God's mission and character since, as followers of Jesus, serving that mission is our priority. But they also must represent the voice and needs of the people to God, negotiating on their behalf. Organizational leaders that don't hear and respond compassionately to the needs of their employees (when offered with integrity) may never move their organizations forward in productivity even if they have a perfectly crafted mission statement. Organizations do not exist without their employees. Churches do not exist without their congregations. Communities do not thrive without their constituents striving together for the benefit of their neighborhood. Prophet-leaders must build bridges of mutual understanding—enabling God to hear the cries of God's people, and God's people to understand the heart, call, and plans of God.

---

15. Solomon, "10 Rules," para. 7.

Rule #5: With Grief and Loss, It's Personal, Not Just Business

When the writer of the letter to the Colossians faced into the challenges of the first-century church's experience of internal conflict, external persecution, and the existential angst bridging the two, he didn't respond dismissively with, "hey, it's just what comes with the territory of being a follower of Jesus." Instead, he recognized that within a culture where there are more reasons to stay disconnected than there are to unite, it's best to change our perspective. He wrote, "So if you have been raised with Christ, seek the things that are above, where Christ is, seated at the right hand of God. Set your minds on things that are above, not on things that are on earth, for you have died, and your life is hidden with Christ in God. When Christ who is your life is revealed, then you also will be revealed with him in glory" (Col 3:1–4).

As followers of Jesus, we need to remember who we are, why we're here, and to where God is leading us. That's the mosaic view. Loss hurts. It's personal. We must be honest, transparent, vulnerable with our emotions within and around our losses. And we need to be empathetic with others as they go through their losses.[16] Doing so, our losses unite us within God's redemptive story, a story that takes us to the cross of Christ. And Jesus's death was very personal.

Rule #6: Grief Is Best Approached with Improvisation

Prophet-leaders respond to what's presented to them—whether from God, or from the circumstances around them. They are uniquely wired to interpret what they see considering the word of God, and then to move both people and organizations into aligning with that word. Situations of loss, however, remind us that we are never fully in control of life. Improvisation teaches us that control is an illusion. People die. Bad decisions may produce negative results. Good decisions may lead to new expectations that require letting go of old paradigms or structures. Changes occur. Grief happens. Rather than trying to react, we need to learn how to *respond*—fluidly, and in tandem with the Holy Spirit.

In my previous book, *Mission Rift*, I argued that conflict is best embraced with the skills of improvisation, and I offered parameters and

---

16. Cochran, "Most Important Rules."

principles to help leaders do so.[17] Reframing some of those parameters and principles of improvisation to the processes of loss and grief, we can reorient our bargaining strategies as we negotiate with our pain or plead on behalf of God's people. For example, as followers of Jesus, we need to suspend our old way of thinking that death and endings are "bad" and that the life we currently have is "good." Rather, our faith tells us that death has lost its "sting," that in the grand "mystery" of God's design, "we will all be changed," that when the trumpet sounds, "the dead will be raised imperishable, and we will be changed. . . . For this perishable body must put on imperishability, and this mortal body must put on immortality. . . . When this perishable body puts on imperishability, and this mortal body puts on immortality, then the saying that is written will be fulfilled: 'Death has been swallowed up in victory'" (1 Cor 15:51–55). That belief can give us strength to face into our losses—both personal and corporate—with confidence in God's ultimately redemptive plan.

With improvisation, we may be able to approach our bargaining with *curiosity* rather than control, with flexibility rather than fear—asking questions of our pain, of our loss, or even of God, but doing so with a vulnerability to what God may be doing to redeem the moment: "I lift up my eyes to the hills—from where will my help come? My help comes from the Lord, who made heaven and earth" (Ps 121:1–2); "O Lord, I have heard of your renown, and I stand in awe, O Lord, of your work. In our own time revive it; in our own time make it known; in wrath may you remember mercy" (Hab 3:2). As with the psalmist and the prophet, our confidence in engaging loss with improvisation comes with a deep abiding assurance that God loves us, that we can trust that God has our best in mind, that God is caring for us as God is carrying out the grander plan of the divine mosaic.

So, with curiosity, we can listen not only *to* our pain, but *into* our pain—for the penetrating presence of our incarnational Lord who has promised to be with us (Matt 28:20). Then, we can respond to what comes our way in any given moment—responding with a mosaic faith that God's got this, that God's got us, that God's got me, even when we don't feel it. Often, I'll pray, "So, Lord, what are you doing? What are you up to that I'm just not seeing yet?" Rather than jumping in and renegotiating the deal to meet my need to control a given situation (which clearly is my defensive "go-to" strategy), I've been trying to lean into my losses—asking *my losses* how I should respond. What I'm learning in my grief is that I am to be

---

17. See Woolverton, *Mission Rift*, chapter 9.

fully present in the moment—fully acknowledging what I'm feeling in that moment, naming out loud what I'm sad or angry or depressed about within that particular situation. Then I am to allow what I have named to become my bargaining voice, appealing solely to the goodness of our incarnational God, and trusting God with the outcome. It's not quid pro quo at all. It's trusting solely in God's gracious gift of God's incarnational presence to heal, redeem, and provide hope.

A prayer that I have taught my current congregation, and which I have been using personally during my own seasons of loss, helps to frame out this improvisational approach to grief: "Lord, what do you need me to see, what do you need me to hear, what do you need me to know, and what do you need me to do? I am your servant, in Jesus's name. Amen." All of life is held in the embrace of God's grace. If I can trust God with my life, then I must believe that I can trust God with my pain.

BARGAINING WITH YOURSELF

Bargaining is never easy when it comes to grief and loss. While it certainly can give voice to our pain, frustration, and helplessness, it can also provide us with incredible information about our loving God, as well as about ourselves. When I have sufficient space to reflect on my losses, I am striving to ask more *from* my losses than just being the recipient of the pain of grief they bring. If I am to negotiate with my pain—or the pain of those that I lead and care about—then, in some way, I want to negotiate more aggressively when it comes to what my losses have to teach me. For example:

- What specifically is my situation of loss teaching me about who I am, what I believe, in what or in whom I place my trust and hope?
- What is my loss exposing in me of things about my character for which I am embarrassed or ashamed, or uniquely proud? What has it caused me to see of my limitations, my ambitions, my mission, my comfort within the liminal periods of life?
- What is my loss teaching me about my view of God—as Provider, as Lord, as Savior, as Redeemer, as Tester, as Taker, as Grace-Giver?
- If my loss is taking something important from me, then what can I demand from my loss? As I emerge from this loss, what have I gained from it? From what has such a loss given me freedom?

- From this loss, what have I received that I now must give away to others—gifts of hope to ease their journey from one who has been there?

As with Hannah—and Sarah, Manoah's wife, Elizabeth, and Mary—it is within the human constraints of loss that we hear the cry of a baby, born amid pain to remind us of the plans of a redeeming God. Within impossible scenarios, God reveals the possible. Prophet-leaders bear within the womb of God's word the message of hope and reconciliation, not just of judgment. God's invitation is always to cast our view to the grander mosaic where we will see not only deliverance, but resurrection and recreation. Bargaining leads us into the reality of our losses—into the deeper waters of our grief so that we may discover that grander design and its presentation of new life.

Yet, bargaining has a close companion to assist us on that pathway toward discovery. And this companion is not easy to negotiate with on our own. That companion is depression, and it is both a stumbling block and a blessing to the prophet-leaders who grieve for themselves and their people. The prophet Huldah will mentor us into the darker corners of our journey.

A Prophet in Time: Huldah

Can a person know that they are going to die and not lament the life they leave behind . . . not regret the choices that have shaped their journey away from the heart of Adonai?

Huldah's thoughts were interrupted by her husband's repeated question: "Huldah, are you not listening? *Ishti*? I was just talking to you, are you not going to answer?"

"I'm sorry, Shallum." Huldah had been standing by the window, staring out at the Temple Mount, lost in thought. The vision that had awakened her during the night, and the word that was coming to her from Adonai since dawn, were strong and deeply disturbing. Once again it appeared that she would need to be the bearer of Adonai's message of judgment, portraying Adonai's deep disappointment in the congregation of Judah. Their sin—their chronic idolatry, in particular—was such an affront to the Most High.

Huldah certainly knew that Adonai understood the human propensity to rebel, choosing their own path rather than the path laid out so clearly in the Torah. The witness of the Torah showed Israel's recalcitrance most especially—even from the very moments when Moses was receiving the law, when the people of Israel danced before a golden calf and acted more like the Egyptians from whom they had fled than the people called by Adonai's name. Not much had changed since then with the vacillating character of Adonai's chosen ones. Rebellion was in their blood, and their lustful appetites for independence from their Creator never strayed far from the ways of Babel or Sodom. It deeply burdened Huldah—this rift between humanity and the One who so passionately pursued them.

Yet, to consistently violate the covenant of first love that had defined Adonai's heart for the children of Israel? No . . . judgment was now coming. Huldah could hear it in the Voice that poured Adonai's word into her mind. She could *feel* it in that accelerating rift that burdened her soul, forcing itself to come forth in pronouncements that she was reluctant to utter due to the intense grief that it exposed in her. It was impossible not to come, though. It was the law of sowing and reaping after all, she reasoned. What is sown in unrighteousness will reap the ramifications consistent with unrighteousness. The judgment was Judah's own fault. They caused their own destiny. Make no mistake, she thought, the Mighty One will not be mocked.

In last night's vision, Huldah had seen the discovery of the "book of the Law"—a copy of the words of Moses reminding the people of Israel to remain faithful to Adonai as they prepared to enter the promised land. According to her vision, Hilkiah, the high priest, was thinking that this discovery was a coincidence, but Huldah knew that the timing was specific to Adonai's plan. Adonai wanted King Josiah to hear the words that potentially would reclaim the heart of the people and she hoped they would hear it and respond before it was too late.

Yet, she knew from what she saw last night that it was too late for many—for she saw devastation coming upon the people of Judah. She saw the violation of the Most Holy Place, the desecration of the holiest sections of the sanctuary. She saw the theft of the sacred vessels of worship, and the violent destruction of the temple itself. She saw the slaughtering of many lives from the invading forces of Babylon. She saw the eviction of the people from their homes and the exile of many to the land of the invaders. And she saw it all as if it had already happened. Not a good sign when it came to her prophetic visions. The images were overwhelming her—because she knew that her people would not heed the warnings.

"Are you okay? You seem miles away with your thoughts. What's wrong? Are you having another one of your visions?" Shallum stared at his wife for the longest time awaiting a response, finally looking away when he was greeted by Huldah's downcast countenance and silence as she turned from the window toward him. He had seen that face before. Whatever she had seen—it wasn't going to be good news. Something was weighing her down, something devastating. He just knew it, and it raised his own anxiety. Sometimes her visions from Adonai had a way of taking her to very dark places emotionally, they burdened her so.

"They'll be coming today, I'm sure." Huldah broke the protracted silence.

"Who? Who's coming today?"

"The high priest. And several others. From the king." She spoke with casual, almost resigned tones, as if she had been expecting this envoy for days.

"What? Hilkiah is coming . . . *here*?" From his chair at the table, Shallum looked quickly about the room assessing all that needed to be put in order and cleaned up prior to such a visit. "What time? Do we have enough food for them?"

"No, Shallum," Huldah responded compassionately to her husband's anxiety. "No need to trouble yourself. I shall meet them at the temple gate where I usually go to pray. When they seek me, I'll be there waiting for them."

It was after *minchah*, the afternoon hour of prayer, when Hilkiah, the high priest, along with the representatives of the king—Ahikam, son of Shaphan, Achbor, son of Micaiah, Shaphan, the secretary, and the king's servant, Asaiah—arrived at the temple gate where Huldah was known to pray and prophesy. Many leaders over the years—prophets, priests, and kings—had either come to her in this spot or had sent envoys on their behalf, inquiring from her the wisdom of Adonai within various situations. Her words had power. Her insights were rarely questioned. Her prophesies were often devastatingly accurate. These leaders consistently deferred to her, and thus she wielded great influence over religious and government officials alike—an influence that she dispensed with great humility.

Truth be told, Huldah did not shy away from being the vessel through whom Adonai would speak both words of hope and invitation as well as confrontation and judgment. She long ago had shed the prideful hold on power and influence that so many had craved, and instead endured the tempering of the Spirit as Adonai's word singed the edges of her appetites for such things. Rather, Huldah held her prophet's role at arm's length, realizing that even in the worst moments of prophetic judgment, she too was a recipient of Adonai's message, not just its dispenser. The daunting task of hearing and seeing—and *feeling*—such potent images from Adonai in advance of everyone else often kept her on her knees in heartbroken lamentation as she grieved for the people of Judah, *her* people, and the impact her words would have. She knew that she, too, was guilty by association, implicated by birth into this ethnic tribe, though not personally complicit with the choices of her Hebrew siblings. The sins of Israel and Judah were her sins though, for she was—and *is*—Israel and Judah, part of the congregation of Adonai's chosen ones. And that made what she was about to reveal even more difficult.

The entourage approached from the left, forming a semicircle around Huldah. She was kneeling on a small rectangular mat made from flax. The mat had been severely frayed around the edges, and significantly weathered by many years of being used in the midday sun. Her eyes were closed in prayer. Her hands were gently placed on her lap, palms turned up, one atop the other, with her fingers slightly curled as if they were holding onto something. She could sense the men's presence by the shadows they cast over her and her prayer mat.

"I know why you're here," Huldah said, her eyes still closed.

"We would speak with you, Huldah, on behalf of the king." It was Hilkiah, his address rehearsed and spoken before he realized what Huldah had said.

Huldah smiled a slight, warm smile as she opened her eyes and looked at the group of men around her. She genuinely liked Hilkiah, but also liked anticipating what he was going to say, and then creating a path forward in the conversation just one step ahead of him.

"The Book of the Law that you found . . . did you read it?" She knew the answer, of course, but asked anyway. She wanted the men to know that she knew—to give further credential to what she was about to reveal.

"Yes, we have." Hilkiah was surprised by her question since no one else knew about the discovery, but he responded on behalf of the group. "And Shaphan read it to the king. It was the king that sent us to inquire of Adonai."

Getting on her feet, Huldah looked at each of the men in turn, pausing to make eye contact to create a link between her and them and the words she was about to share, that they too might feel the weight of the prophetic message.

"Thus says Adonai, the Mighty One of Israel," Huldah began. "Tell the man who sent you to me, Thus says the Lord, I will indeed bring disaster on this place and on its inhabitants—all the words of the book that the king of Judah has read. Because they have abandoned me and have made offerings to other gods, so that they have provoked me to anger with all the work of their hands, therefore my wrath will be kindled against this place, and it will not be quenched. But as to the king of Judah, who sent you to inquire of the Lord, thus shall you say to him, Thus says Adonai, the Mighty One of Israel: Regarding the words that you have heard, because your heart was penitent, and you humbled yourself before Adonai, when you heard how I spoke against this place, and against its inhabitants, that they should become a desolation and a curse, and because you have torn your clothes and wept before me, I also have heard you, says Adonai. Therefore, I will gather you to your ancestors, and you shall be gathered to your grave in peace; your eyes shall not see all the disaster that I will bring on this place."[1]

The men were silent for quite some time, taken aback by the potency and directness of Huldah's words. At one point, Hilkiah opened his mouth to speak, but he was at a loss. How does one respond to a message of such severe judgment? How does one react to the wrath of the Mighty One?

It was only after the silence became rather awkward that Huldah spoke. "Is there anything else I may do for you?" It wasn't that she was uncompassionate to the fact that these men were taken by the devastating news of the message. Rather, it was because she was still overwhelmed by her own prophecy—still processing the images from her vision. Indeed, she spared the men the graphic details of what she had seen. Yet, she had been reliving those images since they were first revealed to her. The scenes played repeatedly in her mind causing her to go deeper and deeper into her grief on behalf of her people, on behalf of her family. They would all pay a severe price.

"We will take this message back to the king," Hilkiah said, finally regaining his words. "Uh . . . thank you. Shalom." His voice trailed off as he turned and walked away, not even waiting for the others in his entourage. Silently, one by one the other men followed suit, progressively dissipating the shadows that had previously blanketed Huldah and her prayer mat and leaving Huldah in the vacuum brought by her own words.

---

1. 2 Kgs 22:15–20, modified by me.

4

Depression

Power is most effective when it is shared.

She declared to them, "Thus says the Lord, the God of Israel: Tell the man who sent you to me, Thus says the Lord, I will indeed bring disaster on this place and on its inhabitants—all the words of the book that the king of Judah has read."

—2 Kings 22:15–16

Job's friends should have quit while they were ahead. Eliphaz the Temanite, Bildad the Shuhite, and Zophar the Naamathite, did an amazing job caring for Job considering his great suffering—at least, at the start.

First, *they showed up*. In Job 2:11–12 we read that Job's friends "met together to go and console and comfort him. When they saw him from a distance, they did not recognize him, and they raised their voices and wept aloud; they tore their robes and threw dust in the air upon their heads." Clearly, Job had a few good friends. They heard about Job's calamities, left their homes, joined up together, and went to support him. When they saw him, it says that "they did not recognize him." Can you not picture that? Job had lost everything he had. He lost his children. Now, his body was suffering from "loathsome sores" so badly that nothing, not even trying to scratch himself with a potsherd, was helping (2:7–8). So, he "sat among the ashes"—an outward sign of significant grief (2:8). His physical appearance bore testimony to the emotional pain he felt, such that his friends, from a distance, could palpate his grief. They "raised their voices and wept aloud" and they "tore their robes and threw dust in the air upon their heads" (2:12). These were ancient rituals of grief, culturally significant methods of grieving together within community. Never underestimate the power of showing up, of outwardly grieving with those who are important to us.

Second, *they shut up*. Verse 13 says, "They sat with him on the ground for seven days and seven nights, and *no one spoke a word to him*, for they saw that his suffering was very great" (italics mine). Whether it was intentional or not, their ministry of presence provided hope to Job, reminding him that he was not alone despite how isolating his losses made him feel. I call this ministry of presence *accidental pastoral care*—care that does not depend on what we say, but on who we are and who we represent. For me, accidental pastoral care is sacramental. It is an outward and tangible sign of an inward and spiritual truth that reminds those who are hurting of the incarnational nature of God's presence. When we are suffering, there's incredible power in knowing—in feeling—that we're not alone.

STUPID IS WHAT STUPID SAYS

Then the friends got stupid. In chapter 3, Job does what we all do when we're suffering and feel that our pain is unfair—he vents. In loss, sometimes we lash out and get angry. That's grief. Once we leave the numbness of our denial we plunge into the reactive phase of anger. Maybe even multiple times. Venting is our way of crying out. Even when we demand answers to our "why me?" questions, mostly we're simply giving voice to our pain as we search for someone or something to blame for how we feel. In our grief process, that's our way of trying to regain a sense of agency within what feels out of control, confusing, and chaotic.

Hearing Job's venting causes Eliphaz to give theological responses to Job's existential diatribe—"If one ventures a word with you, will you be offended? But who can keep from speaking?" (4:2). And his responses were typical examples of what people might say in response to someone else's grief—both the people of Job's day, as well as for us today: "You can't be totally innocent, can you? You must have done something to anger God to bring about such punishment" (my paraphrase of Job 4). One by one, Job's friends join in on the debate—putting Job on the defensive and needing to justify his righteous standing before the Lord.

DEPRESSION

Job's friends got stupid. I know that's a harsh word, for we all have been "stupid" at some point when faced with the profound grief of those we care about. My dear friend Lisa, who lost her eight-year-old daughter Kelly to brain cancer, once told me that while in the receiving line at the funeral, a person said, "God must have needed another angel, so he took Kelly." My friend Joan, who lost her son, Alex, in a tragic car accident told a similar story: "At least, you have two other children." Clearly unhelpful—and truly bad theology. When faced with the raw, painful realities of loss, meaningful people get stupid. We don't know what to say, so we contrive statements that, in the moment, make *us* feel better by easing *our* anxiety, even though they don't help the person grieving. Many months after those respective funerals, Lisa, Joan, and I presented a message to the church on how to respond to those who are grieving—what to say, what not to say, what to do that's helpful, what not to do because it's not helpful. I still remember those words of advice from these two incredible women of faith. Truly, we cannot judge those who have not been taught to act differently.

Job was not looking for a theological debate—even if doing so assisted him in venting further. Job was not looking for someone to tell him that he was responsible for his pain, that he was the cause of his loss. Job was angry and depressed—and his depression was not tolerated by his friends. Something, dare I say it, that we're all guilty of at times.

Listen to what he says in Job 6:2–13.

> O that my vexation were weighed,
>   and all my calamity laid in the balances!
> For then it would be heavier than the sand of the sea;
>   therefore my words have been rash.
> For the arrows of the Almighty are in me;
>   my spirit drinks their poison;
>   the terrors of God are arrayed against me.
> Does the wild ass bray over its grass,
>   or the ox low over its fodder?
> Can that which is tasteless be eaten without salt,
>   or is there any flavor in the juice of mallows?
> My appetite refuses to touch them;
>   they are like food that is loathsome to me.
> 'O that I might have my request,
>   and that God would grant my desire;
> that it would please God to crush me,
>   that he would let loose his hand and cut me off!
> This would be my consolation;

> I would even exult in unrelenting pain;
>   for I have not denied the words of the Holy One.
> What is my strength, that I should wait?
>   And what is my end, that I should be patient?
> Is my strength the strength of stones,
>   or is my flesh bronze?
> In truth I have no help in me,
>   and any resource is driven from me.

Have you ever been depressed due to the layers of grief upon your heart? I have.

MY DEPRESSION STORY

A month after my heart attack (see the introduction to this book), I began my requisite twelve weeks of cardiac rehab. Three times a week, wearing my sweats and sneakers, I would show up at the hospital where I had received my life-changing diagnosis. I'd get off the elevator on the cardiac floor (where I had been a patient for four days), feeling myself tense up with the post-traumatic stress that inevitably would trigger palpitations, and talk myself into walking the hallway to the cardiac rehab center. There, I would put on heart monitor leads, don a hospital gown, and head over to the treadmills to begin my regimen of supervised exercises. In truth, I was not that out of shape. For years, I had played racquetball at least twice a week. Sure, I was thirty-five pounds overweight, but hey, church fellowship meals—need I say more? My heart attack had damaged my heart muscle, though, and the rehab was meant to help me strengthen what needed to be strengthened—in my body as well as my mind. I needed to know the limits of what I could do.

Once I got started with my exercises, I was okay. My mind kicked into gear, and I was able to adjust to the surroundings. "I can do this," I would say to myself. I was the guy, after all, who did a wedding ceremony the weekend after I got out of the hospital. (Obviously, denial provides multiple ways for us humans to be stupid!) In time, my personality even came out. By week four, I was no longer the new guy in rehab. I'm an encourager, by nature, so I became the encourager at rehab—coming alongside those who were new and voicing support: "You've got this! You can do it! I know that this feels daunting right now, but you'll see progress soon. I'm praying for you." Despite the setting, I was able to be me—*Pastor* Dave—and that ultimately helped my brain get out of its own way toward healing.

Then one day, during my sixth week, I was doing my thing on the treadmill—the middle one of three lined up next to each other. The treadmill on my left and the one on my right were each occupied by men who, by their own admission, were in their early eighties. They were cross-talking with each other around me. At one point, each of them began to share the list of medicines that they were on because of their heart issues, as well as all the side effects that they were experiencing. With each drug that they named, I remember saying to myself, "I'm on that. I'm on that. I'm on that one too . . ."

In that single moment, I let out an expletive under my breath. My forty-one-year-old body and mind felt overwhelmed and incredibly old. It felt as if a massive weight suddenly came onto my shoulders and it was pulling me down, deep into an abyss of despair. A wave of anxiety hit me hard and I needed to get out of there. I hit the "stop" button on the treadmill, went to the changing room, disconnected my wires, ripping the lead patches off my chest, got dressed as fast as I could, and made a beeline to the elevator. I made it to my car in the parking lot and just started weeping: "God, is this what I'm in for? Is this what my life is going to be like?" I punched my steering wheel as I punctuated my questions to God.

THE RUNNER'S WALL

Marathoners would know this as the "runner's wall." When it occurs while running, it's usually at that point when your body has depleted over two thousand calories, typically after running for at least two hours or twenty-plus miles in a twenty-six-mile marathon. When it hits, your breathing becomes intensely labored, and you just want to give up.[1] The runner's wall is both physical and mental. Convincing yourself to move beyond the wall can be a challenge—especially while you're still in the race. I had hit my proverbial wall. I continued going to rehab, but for the next several weeks the wind was out of my sails. I went because I had to, not because I had a vision of myself becoming healthy and restored.

But God never leaves us in our despair. Around week ten, a new patient came into the rehab unit. He was younger than I was, just by a few years. I remember that he looked scared, tentative about starting his journey—much like I had felt my first day. My heart went out to him. Once he got connected to his monitors and began his routine, I came up alongside of him and began encouraging him: "You've got this! You can do this! This

---

1. DiChiara, "Runner's Wall."

is week ten for me, and I'm better today than I was on day one. We're all here to help you." With each session, I saw him make progress. Helping him helped me to finish up my twelve weeks. I had learned a lot about my body, for sure, but I also learned a lot about me.

After rehab, I started walking every morning at the local mall. I became one of the many mall-walkers who would show up around 8:00 a.m., before the mall would open to the public, and we would walk the one-mile interior circuit as many times as needed to reach our individual goals. I did it faithfully prior to heading to work. I was feeling much better physically than I had been, though I knew I was not over my "wall" experience. That weight just never seemed to go away. In fact, it was getting bad enough that I was starting to have panic attacks out of the blue. The first one happened when I was in a theater watching a movie. Normally, I love movies. But this panic attack made me get up and leave the theater. It felt like the walls were closing in on me. So, I went to see my doctor.

"Dave, I think maybe you're depressed," he offered, tentatively.

"Depressed?" Me? I counseled people who were depressed. Normally, I'm a glass-half-full kind of guy. Depressed?? "This just doesn't make sense to me, doc. I'm the epitome of a non-anxious guy."

"It's understandable," my doctor friend continued. "After all, you had a life-changing event that required you to face your mortality."

"I faced my mortality a long time ago," I replied. "I'm not afraid of death."

"What are you afraid of then?" My doctor's question was incredibly insightful, and it made me think. After a moment, I replied.

"I'm afraid of limitations. I don't want to die before I die."

Trying to be helpful, my doctor prescribed an antidepressant. After taking just one pill, I had a significant sensitivity reaction, producing a diagnosis of being serotonin sensitive. So, no pills. I had to figure out another way.

OFF MY GAME

My panic attacks continued and even intensified. I felt so totally off my game, worried that at any moment another attack would occur. I began to add layers to my preparations "just in case"—making sure that I knew where exits were in any building I entered, locating the nearest hospitals when my wife and I were traveling, just to be prepared. My anxiety was now making me obsessive and compulsive. Clearly, something was wrong, but I didn't know what. If I wasn't depressed before, I definitely was becoming depressed now.

My gut was telling me that I was having side effects to the medicines I was now on. Patiently, my cardiologist tried changing out my panel of meds, what I called my "cardiac cocktail," one at a time, working with me to see if there was any improvement. Back then, I'm sure that my doctors were concerned, but I do think that they believed my issues were mental health related rather than medical.

Admitting defeat, I finally decided to put myself into counseling. I am very well networked with counselors in my area. Many of them are good friends. I wanted someone who would not be biased however, so I went off my grid and chose a counselor I did not know personally in an agency that I deeply respected.

After several sessions, the counselor intuitively said, "Dave, you're an insightful person with great intuition. What do *you* think is going on?"

"I think I'm having a side effect to one of the medicines that I'm on. I just don't know which one. I've tried switching them out with my cardiologist for the past several months, but I still have the same reactions. It's incredibly frustrating and I just want to give up." Whether he thought my idea was credible or not, he validated me by asking, giving me a sense of agency in a time when I felt dissociated from my sense of normal.

PLEADING WITH GOD

My symptoms continued to worsen though. I was having multiple panic attacks throughout the day, and anxiety was consuming me. It hit a peak on the evening of Kristine's birthday. We were slated to go out for dinner, and I barely made it through the meal. We got home, she went to bed, and I poured out my heart before the Lord. On my knees, I begged God to give me wisdom. I quoted scriptures like James 1:5—"If any of you is lacking in wisdom, ask God, who gives to all generously and ungrudgingly, and it will be given you." Exhausted, I then headed up to bed.

My bedtime routine included spraying my nose with a prescription nasal steroid spray because of chronic allergies. I had just gone to the pharmacy that day to get the new bottle. As I pulled the bottle out of its box, the paper insert that describes all the drug properties and side effects popped out and onto the floor. Normally, I just throw those out. As I picked it up, a voice inside of me said, "Read it." Sitting down on the edge of the toilet, I read this tiny pamphlet. There in fine print, under the heading "side effects," I read all my symptoms. It began to make sense to me. Somehow, this normally "topical" steroid had been impacting my systems, causing my symptoms, causing my panic attacks. Through tears on my toilet, I thanked God.

A visit to my doctor confirmed that the steroid was somehow leaking into my bloodstream, causing major sensitivity reactions. At least that was the tentative diagnosis. Since it was a steroid and I had been on it for some time, I weaned myself off. Within two weeks, the panic attacks disappeared and the weight on my shoulders lightened.

My depression did not completely dissipate though. In fact, the existential nature of living with heart disease and the limitations it has caused, plus the repeated journey of navigating medicines that have depressive side effects (like beta blockers and certain cholesterol drugs) and regulating lifestyle choices that make me feel older than I want to admit I am, has kept me dealing with a low-grade depression ever since.

To this day, I have been living out some of the real-time limitations that I had told my doctor that I feared more than death. But I am immensely better than I had been. With the Holy Spirit's daily companionship, I have adapted. I'm a prophet-leader, after all. Every day, I look for the ways the Spirit is speaking into my journey. I look for things for which to be thankful. And I have continued to look for how my experiences might reflect the call that God has placed on my life. I have chosen to live in the moment and to cast my eyes on what the Spirit wants to reveal. I begin each day and end each day with the following affirmation of faith: "Lord, I trust you. I know you love me, and I love you. Thank you for using me today. Redeem the day." I choose to live every day by God's grace, not worrying (so much) about tomorrow, but staying focused on today. Of course, my experiences have taught me more than I ever wanted to know about empathy. As a leader, unfortunately, I needed to learn that lesson the hard way.

Some leaders have it worse.

FUNCTIONAL AND EXISTENTIAL DEPRESSION

There are many leaders all over the world who have navigated the difficult waters of depression for years. Some simmer with what psychologists have called *functional depression* (or *high-functioning depression*). Functional depression (officially, now called persistent depressive disorder, when diagnosed) is quite common. It affects nearly 1.5 percent of adults in the United States, by today's statistics.[2] It's a chronic undercurrent of low-level feelings

---

2. Amatenstein, "Dilemma," para. 3.

of depression that do not necessarily debilitate a person's abilities to function within daily life. For many, friends, family, neighbors, and coworkers might not even notice that anything is wrong. That's because high-functioning depression can affect high-functioning people—like leaders—who simply push through their emotions as they pursue their goals and give the impression that nothing is wrong.

Alongside of functional depression in leaders, I have seen what is called *existential crisis*, or its partner, *existential depression*.[3] This is a relatively modern understanding of certain types of mood disorders that typically don't fit into any of the other classifications of depression. In fact, it's not an official diagnosis. It's a compilation of emotions, mood responses, or critical reactions connected with facing into any radical change within a person's life—the kind of change that searches for deeper meaning and purpose.[4] It's the kind of depression that grief often brings.

Within the context of this book, I would say that existential crises can occur when leaders become fully aware that they are living a life that is outside the parameters of their identity, their call, their passions, their abilities, or their gifts, or have faced a loss of significant impact, and they feel powerless to do anything about it. When that crisis is not addressed appropriately, or the crisis moves from an acute phase to a chronic phase, the leader can become depressed.

While I have a degree in psychology, intensive training within critical care and trauma, and over thirty-five years of experience providing pastoral counseling and support, I will go on record saying that I am not a clinical psychologist, nor do I want to pretend to be. I'm not here to give diagnoses, nor will this book rival the *Diagnostic and Statistical Manual of Mental Disorders* in giving the differentials of depression. I would like to share with you, however, what I have learned about depression as applied to grief in the lives of leaders within the contexts of Christian ministry and organizational settings.[5]

First, we need a working definition.

---

3. Cassata, "Existential Depression."

4. For more on this, see Berra, "Existential Depression."

5. Obviously, depression has many causes, some of which involve biochemical, pharmacological, and other medical bases. In this chapter, I am using the term specifically to reflect the emotional processes connected with grief and loss. Individuals dealing with depression and its related symptoms should be advised to consult with a professional counselor or medical personnel when more formal diagnoses and treatments are required.

A PROPHET-LEADER'S DEFINITION OF GRIEF-RELATED DEPRESSION

As I've shared throughout this book, grief is our normal human reaction to change. The more intense the change is, the more intense the grief response will be. Remember my axiom from the introduction? *A catalyst produces change. Change produces transition. Transition produces loss. Loss produces conflict. Always.* Sometimes that conflict is internal, inside the mind and heart of the leader.

Fundamentally, grief is about loss. In her book *Death: The Final Stage of Growth*, Elisabeth Kübler-Ross wrote, "Dying is something we human beings do continuously, not just at the end of our physical lives on this earth."[6] And our anxiety around facing death in its various forms, I contend, is at the root of grief's depression.

From a prophet-leader's perspective on grief, my working definition of depression is simple: *grief-related depression is our emotional response to situations within which we feel powerless to change the circumstances we desperately want to change.*

Most leaders are fixers. We troubleshoot. We strategize. We envision pathways for expansion. We navigate around obstacles. We forge new roads toward our goals. We just don't typically do endings well. Here are a few examples:

Jane

When Jane's best friend was told that her breast cancer had returned and that there was nothing that could be done, Jane started drinking heavily. They had been best friends since third grade and for the last seven years worked together for the same parachurch ministry that Jane had started. How would she survive this devastating loss?

Harry

Harry served a dynamic church that grew rapidly from two hundred in worship to five hundred in just a few years. He was used to the role of a shepherd-leader, personally evangelizing the community that he served, and priding himself on knowing every member that came in the door on

---

6. Kübler-Ross, *Death: The Final Stage*, 145.

Sunday morning. Doing what he knew how to do was becoming a burden. His elders told him he needed to become more of a CEO, but he didn't know what that meant. He felt trapped but didn't want to disappoint anyone. So, he suffered in silence.

Sam

Sam always doubted her leadership skills. She consistently would see her limitations as being greater than her gifts and abilities. Each time she faced a moment of potential success in a role, she would sabotage herself—forcing herself to fail so that she wouldn't have to live beyond her comfort level and disappoint others. That failure would then cause her to devalue herself.

Eddie

Eddie (not his real name) is a pastor. Recently he posted on social media the following: "I am asking for prayer. I just moved today to a new appointment. New city with no family close by. 30 years in ministry and this is the first time I am all alone . . . and lonely. Really struggling this morning. Thanks for prayers." The good thing is that Eddie reached out for prayer. The sad thing is that his support network was Twitter.

Or how about these biblical expressions of depression:

David

"I am weary with my moaning; every night I flood my bed with tears; I drench my couch with my weeping. My eyes waste away because of grief; they grow weak because of all my foes" (Ps 6:6–7).

David Again

"My God, my God, why have you forsaken me? Why are you so far from helping me, from the words of my groaning? O my God, I cry by day, but you do not answer; and by night, but find no rest" (Ps 22:1–2).

And David Again

"Save me, O God, for the waters have come up to my neck. I sink in deep mire, where there is no foothold; I have come into deep waters, and the flood sweeps over me. I am weary with my crying; my throat is parched. My eyes grow dim with waiting for my God" (Ps 69:1–3).

Elijah

"But he himself went a day's journey into the wilderness, and came and sat down under a solitary broom tree. He asked that he might die: 'It is enough; now, O Lord, take away my life, for I am no better than my ancestors'" (1 Kgs 19:4).

Jeremiah

"My eyes are spent with weeping; my stomach churns; my bile is poured out on the ground because of the destruction of my people, because infants and babes faint in the streets of the city" (Lam 2:11).

When we face something we can't fix, when we've gone beyond our capacities to plow through what's broken, many of us may internalize our emotions. Because we see ourselves as leaders, and perhaps have a perception of ourselves as not wanting to appear vulnerable, we may not ask for help or share our need.

We have too many leaders in our churches and organizations that are hurting—facing seasons of loss and grief either within their own lives, or from walking with those that they care about, or from within the leadership dimensions of their organizations. And it seems that way too often no one is willing to sit with them in their pain. Like Job's friends, we can only tolerate grief for so long—with others or even with ourselves.

In truth, there is a time when leaders must buck up and get moving despite their losses. Wallowing in self-pity doesn't do anyone any good. Yet a failure to acknowledge one's losses, a failure to process those losses in a healthy way, a failure to engage the full range of what those losses beg to teach us, is a choice that just might inevitably sabotage the leadership that God is wanting to shape within us. Our lives, our families, our teams, our churches, our organizations depend on leaders being people of integrity, of vulnerability, of honest character. Like it or not, grief teaches us to be better leaders.

Rightly handling our personal losses will empower our organizations as well—for I would argue that, in addition to leaders, organizations can get stuck in depressive cycles too.

ORGANIZATIONAL DEPRESSION

Let me say that again. I would contend that organizations can be depressed as well. Apparently, I'm not alone in my thinking, either. In her 1991 *Employment Relations Today* article, "Depressed Organizations: Identifying the Symptoms and Overcoming the Causes," business consultant Dr. Lois Frankel agrees. She argues that "entire organizations could be described as depressed, and the patterns of behavior in such organizations are analogous to those observed in depressed individuals."[7] Her article goes on to describe various symptoms and potential causes of organizational depression, making a solid case for her premise.

It makes sense, doesn't it? Organizations are made up of people—a constellation of individuals who, by aspiration or by contract, have aligned themselves under the values, environmental milieu, and mission of that organization. As such, the organization takes on the emotional stories of the people who live under the umbrella of its corporate identity. Within the organization's constantly forming culture, those stories flow both bottom-up and top-down—from employees to management, and from management to employees—influencing the emotional tenor of the environment for all involved. Once established, that culture will reinforce itself, defend itself, and potentially even sabotage anything that threatens to invade its status quo regardless as to whether the system is dysfunctional, or the invading "threat" is missionally advantageous.

AN EXAMPLE

During the summers between my last two years of college and first year of seminary, I had the privilege of working at a motor vehicle inspection station near where I grew up. In New Jersey, most owners took their vehicles to these stations once a year where they would wait, usually in long lines,

---

7. Frankel, "Depressed Organizations," 443.

to see if their cars were in good order according to the state. In classic conveyor belt like fashion, people would take their turn going through various segments of this huge facility where examiners would check everything on their car (lights, steering, brakes, exhaust), pronouncing a "pass" or "fail" by the end of the line.

My first summer, I was the "new guy," so they put me in the least threatening position—making sure that the headlight beams projected to where they needed to be. (As strange as that sounds, there was scientific logic behind the measurements. Just sayin'.) Now, I'm me—an over-responsible, highly efficient, strongly encouraging leader. I was quick on my feet and fast to accomplish what needed to be accomplished. Too fast, apparently. I was getting my cars through my segment of the line too quickly for the other section leaders. It was during my midmorning break that my "mentor" came over to me and said, "You really have to slow things down. We do this job all day, every day. There's no need to rush things." What he was telling me is that there was a cultural rhythm to how things were done there. They all did their jobs well, for sure. But the rhythm of their work was more important than the customer's schedule. The only time that rhythm changed was during the last half hour of the workday, when everyone seemed to rush to get the line done before quitting time, so that no one would need to stay late.

By my second summer, I was now experienced, so they put me into the various other roles in the assembly line. Being back a second year, I was treated more like "one of the guys." Therefore, I had the opportunity to get to know them. These were hardworking, blue-collar men (and one woman), many of whom had been doing this job for decades (one had been there for nearly forty years!). Many of their stories were hard life stories. Often, during the lunch breaks, comments would be shared about management—both in the building as well as at the state level. Clearly, the culture was depressed. Employees did not feel appreciated. Work conditions were often strenuous. I began to realize that their assembly line rhythm itself told a story—a combination of slow-motion ritual as well as some conscious or unconscious passive aggression. The organization was functioning, but was weighed down by an emotionally rhythmic lethargy that came through the culture (and from breathing carbon monoxide, I'm sure!). This culture was passed onto each new generation of employees, an overarching rule that all other employees reinforced.

By my third summer, I was treated like a hero. Rather than just being seen as "one of the guys," I was considered by most to be a friend. I had chosen to come back, to be with them. My encouragement, my positivity even during exhausting days, my penchant for handling angry customers with grace (a foreshadowing of my career in conflict leadership, perhaps?), all seemed to generate warm interactions on the job and off. My humor brought a lightness to our interpersonal interactions. In a way, I had become their chaplain. I genuinely loved them—and based on the farewell they gave me when they knew I would be moving on into my clinical training—they loved me too. The depressive culture seemed more tolerable that summer, though it never really went away. Certainly, some of the employees could have been classified as depressed individually. But I believe that the workplace culture itself was depressed, from the chronic absorption of negative self-value (it's the DMV, for goodness' sake!), reinforced by breathing the air of complaint—and carbon monoxide. The organization was suffering.

Dr. Frankel's article posits that one can assess an organization's corporate mental health by comparing it to patterns exhibited by depressed individuals. It's a truly insightful and helpful premise. However, I'd like to suggest a few additional assessment symptoms based on what I've observed within some of the congregations with whom I have consulted, as well as a few leader-based causes of grief depression within those contexts. I believe these symptoms and causes can be generalized to other organizations as well, since I would contend that organizational depression is rooted in the anxiety caused by unresolved issues of corporate loss and grief—specifically, the loss of a sense of agency or "power" to change one's circumstances.

SYMPTOMS OF GRIEF-RELATED DEPRESSION SPECIFIC TO ORGANIZATIONS

Chronic Conflict

Over the years, I've had the opportunity to come alongside quite a few congregations that were experiencing difficulties—usually reflected in layers of significant conflict. As a rule of thumb, I tend to view conflict as a symptom of something else going on in the systems of the congregation, rather than a primary cause (though there are cases to be made that conflict can have causal agency in certain situations). One of the causes of conflict that I am quick to explore is grief. Grief shows up in many different forms within congregations, but one of the most underexplored is *chronic* conflict. Everyone understands the emotional outbursts and chaotic reactions that can occur when a significant leader or well-loved pastor dies suddenly, or when finances tank and the pressure is on to make ends meet, or when personalities clash around the fact that, for survival, church facilities now must be shared with other congregations. Sudden losses can evoke major acute reactions that play themselves out through displacement within interpersonal arguments and relational friction. But when patterns of repeated conflict can be traced over spans of time, the organizational environment needs to be assessed for causes that are yet unexplored. Unresolved grief is on the top of my list when I'm doing consult assessments—especially when those congregations make references to "the way things used to be," or the facilities show evidence of being a shrine to certain people (e.g., highly visible memorial plaques on the pulpit or communion table), or when certain topics of conversation are quickly dismissed as taboo.

Patterns of Boundary Violations

When organizations have banked a litany of stories related to extramarital affairs, sexual misconduct, and other abuses of power—especially among leadership circles, then unresolved issues of historic or congenital grief may be a cause worth exploring. These externalized behaviors of violation, while certainly reprehensible in and of themselves, may be expressions of internalized anger or a generalized feeling of being out of control within one's domain, not simply rooted in the frames of narcissism or anti-social behavioral diagnoses. When congregations or organizations fail to address these violations, they become complicit with the behavior, often covering it up to maintain emotional distance from the ramifications on the victims. Grief can reveal itself in multiple ways within a mosaic view of life. I would argue that unconfessed sin will show itself as the Holy Spirit pushes up against evil within our faith environments. The ramified effects of the cover-up often become symptomatic with organizational depression.

High Controlling Leaders

In chapter 5 of my book *Mission Rift*, I describe how high controlling people typically are highly anxious and insecure. Often, they are either overcompensating for some other emotional need, or perhaps they are working exceptionally hard at covering up a character flaw. Either way, unresolved grief may play a part in their behind-the-behavior story. Why? Because if these individuals, in fact, are overcompensating or covering up emotions connected to grief, it could be that they are stuck either in denial and unable to face the limits of their abilities, or within the bargaining stage of their process, anxiously trying to placate a "higher power" to regain personal grounding in a season of significant transition. Well, what if those leaders collude with the entire organization to reinforce their behavior? Such collusion occurs when the congregation or organization is gaining sufficient benefit from those leaders as to turn a blind eye to the downsides of their behavior patterns.

Patterns of Sabotage to Self, Project, or Organization

By nature, leaders lead. They tend to thrive on adventure and moving people forward on mission. So, when there are repeated examples of leaders making significant mistakes at pivotal junctures within the organization's growth pattern, such that those mistakes repeatedly prevent the organization or its personnel from attaining growth and productivity, then issues of grief may be at work. A generalized "failure of nerve," to borrow a phrase from rabbi psychiatrist Edwin Friedman,[8] may be rooted in an unwillingness to let go of something in one's past (a role, an emotional security, an ego benefit, a financial gain), or a fear of something in one's future (the ramifications of a promotion, new responsibilities, the need to move one's home). Regardless, such patterns portray avoidant behavior consistent with unresolved grief. Think Jonah and his reactions to God's call for him to preach to Nineveh.

Decompensation

An individual decompensates when, under significant stress, they no longer can cope within the current situation by using their normal defense mechanisms.[9] We often hear it as the person had a mental or emotional breakdown. Organizations, too, can have breakdowns when overloaded by realities beyond their control—such as changes within the economy,

---

8. Friedman, *Failure of Nerve*.
9. "Decompensation."

significant fluctuations in the global market, changes within the community demographics, decline in workforce availability, and lack of infrastructure for supply and demand. In fact, I would argue that our entire US culture decompensated within the challenges of the COVID-19 pandemic—and is still recovering, slowly, from its post-traumatic-stress-induced environment of loss. There are churches that had shut their doors because of COVID-19 and never reopened. There are businesses that closed permanently because of the pandemic's aftermath. Many of those that remained open continue to struggle to this day with getting enough employees to run their businesses. Grief is an underlying source in all these cases.

EXAMPLE CAUSES OF GRIEF-RELATED DEPRESSION IN LEADERS OR ORGANIZATIONS

Whether within individuals, groups, churches, or organizations, grief-related depression can be seen as having any number of causes. Here are several to consider:

The Obvious

- Death of a spouse or partner
- Death of a child
- Getting married
- Separation or divorce
- Your spouse or partner has an affair
- One of the leaders has an affair
- Birth of a child
- Birth of a child with special needs
- A child moves away from home
- A child moves back home after you thought you were empty nesters
- Your child is dating Satan
- Leaving a secular job to pursue ministry
- Your spouse or partner won't attend church

- Decline in physical health
- Illness and/or death of a parent
- Bankruptcy
- Pastoral reassignment or transition of a call
- Not moving to a new church or job when you want to
- Leaving a beloved church or position
- A demotion due to disciplinary action
- Closing a long-tenured family business
- Closing a business due to the ramifications of the COVID-19 pandemic
- Closing a church due to membership and financial declines
- Conflict situations

The Less, or Not-So, Obvious

- Personnel layoffs
- Anxiety around finances
- Retirement
- Betrayal of a staff member
- Firing a staff member
- Not firing a staff member
- Hiring the "perfect" person who turns out to be Satan
- Hiring the "perfect" person who turns out to be better than you
- Members leaving
- The members you wanted to leave, stay
- The church or organization no longer wants you there
- The death or relocation of a significant donor, shareholder, or fundraiser
- Challenges to your character
- The board votes not to give you a raise
- Your child tells you they don't believe in Jesus

- Moving away from friends
- A "promotion"
- Starting a business from the ground up
- Denominational issues
- Changes in the community
- Progressive decline in the demand for your product
- Getting a new boss that doesn't seem to care about you
- Getting a new boss that you don't like
- Poor or hostile working conditions
- Losses caused by a natural (tornado, flood) or human-induced (arson, terrorism) disaster
- Post-traumatic stress, in its various forms and expressions
- Legal actions
- Accusations of sexual misconduct
- Packing up and moving to a new home after the death of a spouse
- Any transition significant to you or the organization

Transitions

The last item on the "less, or not-so, obvious" list perhaps is the most important general category of potential grief-related depression. Indeed, not all transitions are negative. Retirement, promotions, the birth of a baby, getting married, moving out on your own—they all can be seen through the lens of excitement and adventure. Yet, each of these, along with all the truly "negative" transitions of life, have the potential to engage us in the natural rhythms of the grief process—including depression.

My wife, Kristine, retired in 2022 after thirty-three years as a public-school educator. I'm truly proud of her and her accomplishments—most especially in how she was able to be a witness for hope, faith, prayer, and love within her school buildings and among her fellow faculty. Retirement was perfectly timed for her, but it has put her into a season of needing to redefine her role within God's grander design. She retired young with plenty of life left in her to give away when she's ready. In the meantime, her retirement has readjusted our routine, causing us to have to renegotiate the boundaries of our relationship, our family time, our needed personal space (since we're both introverts), as well as the practicalities of when and how to do the rhythms of meals. We've both had to let go of things to take on new dimensions of our relationship.

After spending four years inspiring his church into a turnaround, my good friend Dan received a call to leave the role of senior pastor and to go on staff at a growing megachurch. Giving up the role that had him making all the visionary decisions, crafting his own schedule, and preaching every week, was challenging—even though the new role could not have been more perfectly designed for him. He had to grieve the shift in responsibilities and identity that came with being a senior pastor, not to mention the incredible affirmation he received from the church members who were under his dynamic leadership.

Responding to a call from God to transition out of pastoral ministry, my good friend Sean decided to start up a private practice as a licensed professional counselor—a role for which he had been credentialed previously. Doing a startup counseling business required tons of faith, lots of networking, and an incredible amount of patience to work through the details of building a client base, referral connections, and solid interactions with insurance companies. Leaving the domain of pastoral ministry after serving in that capacity for over fifteen years also required a season of reorientation as Sean redefined his understanding of ministry within God's grander mosaic.

If any of those naturally positive transitions would not have been processed well, Kristine, Dan, or Sean could have found themselves stuck in the depression stage of their grief process. In fact, there are many in their situations who have been depressed because their identities were rooted in what they did, not in who they are apart from their work.

Every time a significant transition occurs—whether positively or negatively viewed—grief is sure to follow. Every time. That doesn't mean that with every transition people sulk and walk around depressed all the time. Most people process through their transitional grief over time depending on the severity of the transition, the emotional capacity of the individuals involved, the process of exiting or ending that has occurred, and how prepared they are in knowing their "next steps plan." People who are "let go" when the termination is unexpected will most likely have a significant grief reaction that will take some time to process. Likewise, companies that lay off blocks of workers may catalyze major depressive episodes not just among the employees who were furloughed, but also among their families, the community where that company resides, those dependent on that company for economic stability, and, what's often missed, the emotional well-being of those who were not laid off, who must remain with increased responsibilities for maintaining productivity.

Faith Community Transitions

Faith communities, as well, can experience transition depression. I grew up in the 1960s and 1970s. The church my family attended was a city church, just on the edge of merging ethnic neighborhoods. In its heyday, it was a relatively large, vibrant Episcopal church, predominantly white, with attendees primarily from the middle to upper middle class. My parents—my dad, a city police officer, and my mom, an emergency room nurse—had been looking for a new church at the time. They had connected with the congregation through the police chaplain. Relatively soon after they joined, a new pastor arrived. That pastor, a white man, was a strong voice for social justice. He had walked with Martin Luther King Jr. in Dr. King's ground swelling march in Alabama. Because of his high commitment to justice and to the "plight of Blacks," our pastor systematically invited more and more Black families from the surrounding neighborhoods to our church. He began preaching against "rich white values" during the time of desegregation, bussing, and racial riots—subsequently offending the majority of the "rich white people" that were left in the pews.

Within a few years the congregation had experienced a significant turnaround in membership demographics. In fact, my family and I, along with a couple other families, were the only white people within what now had become a predominantly Black congregation. Most of the remaining "rich white families" had left the church, and they took their financial support with them. Because of that shift, and because of the complaints made against the pastor by those who had exited, the congregation soon found themselves with another new rector. The new pastor was of an opposite theological framework than his predecessor, and soon he began to offend the Black families that were attending. Within a short time, this once large church now had around fifty people on any given Sunday. Yet another pastor was helped to the exit door. My family was among those fifty who stayed—seeking to build bridges of hope within the dynamically changing neighborhood, under the direction of yet another pastoral leader. The church never recovered, however. In its progressive decline, leaders and parishioners alike had lost the passion to care for the neighborhood, instead moving into a lethargic rhythm of weekly survival until its doors finally closed.

CORE LEADERSHIP GRIEF

I would argue that organizations reflect the emotional state of the core leadership. Organizations in which the core leadership sows compassion, partnership, honesty, integrity, and care for the well-being and safety of their employees reap a harvest of benefits that are mutually sustainable and enriching. However, the reverse is true as well. Core leadership that demonstrates that the bottom line is more important than the employee on the bottom rung of the org chart will reap a harvest that is stressed-out, insecure, and filled with team members who feel like trolls that are trapped in a hostile environment—often leading to depression.

That's why I believe it's critically important for there to be a team approach to that core leadership—a team that includes those prophet-leaders who can have a vision for the future, foster an alignment to the mission, and keep a pulse on the temperature in the room of constituents. For an example, one need only go to any Chick-fil-A restaurant and compare their experience there with that of their own organization or congregation.

Within our faith-based contexts, when one leader has no accountability to others under a shared view of the divine mission, has lots of power and influence, and has a weakened sense of self-awareness, their pride begins to override the skills and abilities that got them to their present position of leadership, and in effect, sets the stage for both decline, identity crisis, and potential moral failure—even if the organization looks healthy and growing on the outside. Remember, functional depression can give the impression that nothing is wrong.

Ultimately, the best way to navigate through the depression stage of grief is by establishing *a culture of shared power* with people of various gifts, perspectives, and visionary sensitivity within the core leadership circles—especially the prophetic. In their article, "Prophets, Priests, and Kings: Re-Imagining Ancient Metaphors of Diffused Leadership for the Twenty-First Century Organization," my good friends Tony Blair and JoAnn Kunz, along with their team of researchers, make the following argument:

> People and organizations are longing for authentic, wise, passionate leaders to guide them toward a better future. And yet, organizations are notoriously suspicious of their prophets. This perceived threat may occur because prophets possess real power that is often exercised liminally (outside of and often in opposition to centralized, positional authority structures), or perhaps because a prophet's highest loyalties are generally invested in the creation of what will or must be, rather than in the conservation of what is. Consequently, an organization's prophets are frequently resisted and often rejected, creating competition between what should be complementary leadership roles, and placing at risk the organization's ability to effectively navigate change.[10]

Blair, Kunz, and their team state that the best forms of leadership are provided when "prophet, priest, and king" are working together in tandem—what they call "Trioptic Typology" in leadership. Leadership, they argue, is at its best when those functions are "diffused throughout an organization, with different individuals or groups performing functions or roles that correspond to these metaphors."[11] Our culture, both inside and outside of the church, they posit, tends to navigate more toward one of the three functions over the others, often valuing that prevailing function based on preference. Blair and Kunz hypothesize that twenty-first-century leadership "will require identification and development of [all] three aspects of leadership within teams of shared leadership throughout an organization."[12] They conclude that "a community functions most effectively when all three roles are explicitly embraced and intentionally inhabited. Conversely, when those roles are not present or are not exercised productively, both the leaders and the organization suffer."[13]

I agree with their overall conclusion—as well as their reflection that the role of the prophet is often misunderstood, misrepresented, or even disenfranchised by many twenty-first century models of leadership. That's a shame. The voice of genuine prophetic leadership is sorely lacking within the culture of our modern organizations—including, ironically, the church. Certainly, we have a large compendium of self-identified prophets that scream at the church and at culture from the sidelines, barking judgments against those who do not conform to their ideologies. But the genuine

---

10. Blair et al., "Prophets, Priests, and Kings," 127–28.
11. Blair et al., "Prophets, Priests, and Kings," 127.
12. Blair et al., "Prophets, Priests, and Kings," 128.
13. Blair et al., "Prophets, Priests, and Kings," 145.

prophetic voice has been pushed aside all too frequently, especially when its call to accountability challenges the visionary leadership of the "king."

Core leadership that values prophetic accountability to the grander mosaic plan of God, engages the constituencies of God's people with compassion and integrity, and fosters apostolic visionary direction within a team that shares power, has the capacity to move stuck, depressed organizations forward on mission, and growing organizations into environments of life-giving generosity and fruit-bearing.

It does the same for the individual leaders as well.

Indeed, *power is most effective when it is given away*. And sharing power is God's counteroffer to the isolating depression of grief. Why? Because there's power in sharing power. Let me explain.

THE POWER IN SHARING POWER

In the context of grief and loss, power is a relative term. Whether we realize it or not, within the new community of Christ, every follower of Jesus has power. Before his ascension, Jesus said to his disciples, "*You will receive power* when the Holy Spirit has come upon you, and you will be my witnesses . . ." (Acts 1:8, italics mine). The apostle Paul wrote to his protégé, Timothy, "For God did not give us a spirit of cowardice, but rather *a spirit of power* and of love and of self-discipline" (2 Tim 1:7, italics mine). Additionally, Paul wrote to the Corinthian church during its season of conflict, "For the kingdom of God depends not on talk but *on power*" (1 Cor 4:20, italics mine). Ephesians 3:20 also reminds us of that same power: "Now to Him who *by the power at work within us* is able to accomplish abundantly far more than all we can ask or imagine" (italics mine). The Holy Spirit, residential in every follower of Jesus, is the very source of power that raised Jesus from the dead (Rom 8:11).

In Greek, one of the primary words used for power is *dunamis*, the root word for our English word "dynamite," or "dynamic." It is used approximately 120 times in the New Testament alone.[14] Many of those references refer to the source of power being God, exercised through the Spirit, at work through or among God's people.

So, within the new community, every Jesus follower has God-given power, through the Spirit that dwells in them. However, not every follower experiences that power in the same way—especially within seasons of loss

14. "Dunamis."

and grief. In our experiences of loss and grief, truly many of us feel *powerless*—unable to change our circumstances or their outcomes, making us feel vulnerable, anxious, confused, and out of control.

However, if we truly believe in the full message of the gospel, and if we sincerely take Jesus at his word—that he has asked God to give his followers "another Advocate" (John 14:16), the "Spirit of truth" that "abides with" us and will be in us (John 14:17), and who is the "Spirit of truth" that will "speak whatever he hears," and "will declare . . . the things that are to come" (John 16:13)—then we must believe that every genuine follower of Jesus has power even within circumstances that are beyond our control.

Truly, we have the power to choose our response to any given situation. We have the power to define our boundaries. We have the power to allow or disallow outside influences to have voice in our lives. We have the power to alter our attitudes. We have the power to forgive or to withhold forgiveness (Matt 6:14–15; John 20:23). We have the power to reframe our reality when it seems that choice has been denied to us (2 Cor 12:9). We have the power to laugh at the bullies that threaten us. We have the power to love our enemies, and to pray for those who persecute us (Matt 5:44). We have the power to place our hope in a day and life that are yet to come, even as we choose to live as if that day and life are already here (Eph 1:20–21).

There's power in our words, for sure—what we say and how we say it. But there's also power in our silence—as we stand silent before our accusers, silent before our fears, and silent before God's amazing grace in the mirrored reflections of our brokenness. There's power in being still, resting in God's presence. There's power in being fully present with ourselves, offering patient grace to our own anxious timeline of chaos. There's power in being fully present with others despite their inability to see us beyond themselves.

For many leaders, power is about control—control of others, of outcomes, of circumstances, of wealth, of behaviors, even of thoughts. The way many of us use power is simply as a cover-up for anxiety. Specifically, we are afraid of being out of control, so we use power to stay in control. Situations of loss threaten us because they force us to face the mortality of our egos, the defenselessness of our existential fears, and the truth that control is an illusion. As stated earlier, depression is our emotional response to situations where we feel powerless to change the circumstances we desperately want to change. Apart from the Holy Spirit, power is simply a false idol of our own narcissism. It is an icon of self-worship. It demands its own way and therefore, as such, it stands antithetical to the gospel of Jesus.

Yet, under the authority of the Holy Spirit, power can become a redemptive instrument of grace during seasons of grief and loss—for those who know how to use it. For prophetic leaders within these contexts, power has four very important qualifiers. First, power requires the boundary of humility. Second, power is strongly rooted within redemptive silence. Third, power can be leveraged in situations of loss, especially in response to injustice. Finally, power can be subversive, challenging everything that seeks to threaten the peace of the Jesus follower.

Power Requires Humility

Within the context of grief and loss, I believe power is a tool. In fact, it must be seen as a tool, rather than as an entitlement, deserved character trait, or inherited limitation or right. As a tool, we must become both aware of power's residential availability to us, as well as adept in its use within a variety of circumstances. We must also be able to apply appropriate boundaries on how we allow it to define us. Otherwise, we will succumb to its idolatrous influences—specifically, that we ourselves are the source of the power.

In Mark 10:35–45, two of Jesus's closest disciples come to him with a power negotiation request: "Teacher," they said, "we want you to do for us whatever we ask of you" (v. 35).

Imagine the audacity—and ignorance—of that moment.

"What is it you want me to do for you?" Jesus asked (v. 36).

They replied, "Grant us to sit, one at your right hand and one at your left, in your glory" (v. 37).

There it was. The classic dilemma: human power versus divine power, human privilege versus servant leadership, self-glory versus self-sacrifice.

"You do not know what you are asking," Jesus said. "Are you able to drink the cup I drink, or be baptized with the baptism I am baptized with?" (v. 38).

"Uh . . . sure!" they answered (v. 39, using here my own paraphrase).

I picture Jesus exasperated by these two friends. According to Mark's Gospel, just moments after sharing with the Twelve a third time about his upcoming betrayal, condemnation, mocking, flogging and death (10:32–34), James and John—the "sons of thunder"—reveal that they have no clue as to what awaits them within the new community despite three years under apprenticeship with Jesus.

These places belong "for those for whom it has been prepared," Jesus replies (v. 40).

And then the other ten disciples hear about what these two did and they "began to be angry with James and John" (v. 41). Wouldn't you? Power plays and other shifts of power engender conflict; and conflict always exposes power disparities.[15]

Snatching yet another teaching moment with the Twelve, Jesus calls them together and says, "You know that among the Gentiles those whom they recognize as their rulers lord it over them, and their great ones are tyrants over them. *But it is not so among you*; but whoever wishes to become great among you must be your servant, and whoever wishes to be first among you must be slave of all" (10:42–44, italics mine).

And to add an exclamation point to the lesson, Jesus adds, "For the Son of Man came not to be served but to serve, and to give his life a ransom for many" (v. 45).

Indeed, in the new community of Jesus followers, everyone has power. Yet as a tool we are to use power judiciously, according to the discipleship values modeled by Jesus, filtered by self-sacrificial love, mediated by grace at the cross of Christ, and respectful of the perfect-tense expressions of the mosaic of others' life stories. In Christ, we must be willing to engage the tool of power for the greater purpose of giving our lives as a ransom for many. It is the way of redemption. It is the way of Jesus.

As prophet-leaders, we must remind ourselves daily that we are shepherds of God's flock. Within our present context, we are not one of the sheep, nor are we to be wolves. Together, it is our responsibility to create safe places for people to encounter Jesus Christ. It is our responsibility to create a safe place for ourselves, as well, through the exercise of healthy boundaries. It is our role to protect and guard, when necessary, the sanctity of those within our care. That's the role of prophetic leadership.

Power as Redemptive Silence

Within grief and loss, one of the most essential expressions of power is silence. Silence speaks volumes. This type of power is not based on position, but on posture; and it is uniquely personal.

---

15. Coleman and Ferguson, *Making Conflict Work*, 83–84.

Depression

While at times silence may mean that one has nothing to say, or is dumbfounded by a moment in time, it may also indicate great inner strength, a self-definition that is independent of the emotional stress of the moment, or a deep abiding trust that God ultimately will redeem the pain of the loss that we feel. As such, our silence is redemptive. It expresses confidence in the mosaic plan of God despite what our circumstances want to tell us.

Jesus's silence before Pontius Pilate, for example, was not a silence based in fear, but in a deep, peaceful, self-defined security and strength that came because he knew who he was, why he was there, and what the divine mission was for him in that moment (Matt 27:11–14). He did not need to defend himself, his reputation, or his rights. He was wholly differentiated from his circumstances while being fully present within them. His silence was powerful.

We don't always feel comfortable in silence, however. Silence exposes vulnerability in us, raising our anxiety. Our need to fill silence says more about us than about our circumstances, more about our anxiety and insecurity regarding our situation, the uncertainty of its potential outcomes, or our discomfort with emotions that we do not know how to express otherwise. As such, often silence threatens our need to be in control of our circumstances, of our destiny, of others who are different than us.

Yet, approaching our losses with silence can be powerful and redemptive. I am reminded of Howard Thurman's book *Jesus and the Disinherited*[16] and the ways that silence and nonviolence "spoke" powerfully into the prevailing culture of racism in the United States. It was Thurman's posture of nonviolence and his use of silence, often embodied within his sermons, that inspired Dr. Martin Luther King Jr. as well as the Civil Rights Movement that they led. Loss was intimately connected with the profound injustices inflicted upon Blacks within America (and the world). As a people group, their "prophetic silence" and nonviolent postures were quite influential in the emerging countercultural movements of the mid-twentieth century. Indeed, the losses experienced by Blacks in America continue to cry out as perfect-tense experiences within our present-tense world.

Similarly, the silent screams of the six million Jews who were incarcerated, tortured, and murdered within the concentration camps of Dachau, Sachsenhausen, Auschwitz, Ravensbruck, and thousands of other camps like them collectively form an affidavit convicting humanity of sins so horrible that neither perpetrator nor bystander want to accept its indictment.

---

16. See Thurman, *Jesus and the Disinherited*.

Their stories speak powerfully from the silence, however, calling humanity to repentance—and to remember and learn.

It is within silence that we may discover the ability to listen—for the thoughts, needs, hurts, griefs, cries of injustice, dreams, and hopes of ourselves and of each other; for the Voice of the Spirit guiding us into the deeper issues of the relationships important to us; for the truth that indeed will set us free from the controlling forces that threaten our well-being; and for the healing that might emerge when we intentionally set aside our right to speak because we trust the One who is Lord even over our chaos.

Power Can Be Leveraged

As leaders therefore, power is to be leveraged for the good of those we are called to serve, since the hallmark of integrity in Christian leadership is that we are called to "shepherd God's flock" (1 Pet 5:1–5; 1 Tim 3:1–13). However, even among faithful followers of Jesus, we live within the constraints of our human condition. Power, indeed, is leveraged—sometimes for the good of all, sometimes for the self-gain of one.

We must choose to use our power judiciously, with humility and grace, to build up the body of Christ, lest we too succumb to the temptation to pool our resources as weapons of mass destruction in order to hide behind our need to control anxiety and pain.

Power can be leveraged via one's confidence of voice. In the face of injustice, a collective voice has the power to draw attention to the plight of oppressed people—regardless of whether the opposing side either (a) is willing to listen, once confronted, and amend behavior and standard practices, or (b) is not inordinately volatile in their use of counter force to subject their people to escalated oppression. Using our prophetic voice is no guarantee that we will be heard, but collectively, it does draw attention to the plight of oppression or to the state of lamentation within which we find ourselves. In fact, doing so might lead to greater oppression, violence, and heartbreak—at least initially, as illustrated historically in the ministries of the biblical prophets, as well as the Black leaders of the Civil Rights Movement. Yet, to not speak the messages given by divine decree for fear of greater losses not only disengages us from the divine mission, which is more important than our pain, but empowers the forces of injustice that we were commissioned to subvert.

The collective voice also can be used negatively within our congregations and organizations. When it draws others into collusion with our pain, with our offense, with our need for revenge, we build a divisive force that ultimately sets believers against each other in a need to "win at any cost." When we experience loss at deep, personal levels, it can unleash the yet-to-be-sanctified forces of our broken human condition and set them antagonistically against what we perceive to be a threat to our well-being—and we will even justify it for ourselves by viewing our actions through lenses of justice, the preservation of the organization, or the pain of what is now owed to us by virtue of our loss.

The power of the collective voice is what nurtures personal pain into corporate action, individual decisions into massive movements. Done well, leveraged power ultimately can be a positive force of transformation, healing, and growth. Yet, when it is handled poorly, people throw away their true power by trying to control others, reacting out of their pain, or lashing out in anger to blame those who hurt them, rather than engaging the transformative voice of personal cross-based influence.

Power is Subversive

Subversion is defined as the "act of trying to destroy or damage an established system or government."[17] Specifically, what we as followers of Jesus are trying to overthrow is the value system of the enemy of love. As Jesus followers, we are called to live as citizens of the new community of Christ here and now, to adopt the values and self-giving behaviors of the One who apprenticed us, and to do so within a society that has yet to figure out it's under new leadership. To be subversive within the new community, power must come under the value system of Jesus. Power, therefore, is most effectual when we give it away—a principle that Jesus modeled himself.

Yet, in a time when mentally disturbed or evil-incarnated people invade the sanctity of our schools with violence, killing innocent children, teachers, and staff, the idea of "giving away power" makes us cringe. Or, what about the continued pandemic of racism that seems to resist extinction despite generations of intentional interventions by those who take stands for racial and ethnic equity? Or, what about global poverty, despite the prevalence of food when resources are governed by political despotism? How do we live prophetically, embodying the message of the cross of Christ,

17. "Subversion."

in the face of such abuses of power, expressions of evil, and reactions of fear? What does the Voice of God have to say to the parents of these young children? To the spouses of these teachers and staff members? To the many who continue to suffer under the oppressions of those who exert power and control? Certainly, justice amid righteous causes is a major theme of the biblical prophets. Ought it not be a theme for us today as well?

Indeed, as prophet-leaders, our power must be leveraged on behalf of the oppressed, provided that we also empower the oppressed to discover their own voice at the table of decision. If we do not, we will establish and reinforce a dependency relationship where the oppressed person or group always needs us to fight their battles. By giving power away to others, we increase their capacity to thrive, not just survive. We provide them the opportunity to speak on their own behalf, as we model love by how we listen to them. We equip them to rise beyond their own (self-)imposed limitations by assuming that they have abilities that are yet untapped, but vitally important to the body of Christ. Perhaps most importantly, we therefore allow ourselves to be receivers of what God has empowered *them* to provide for *our* nurturing, for our benefit, for our growth in Christ, and for the best that God has for the community of faith.

As prophet-leaders, we are to use power to expose what is dark to the light of Christ—first in us, then in the systems, then in the relational dynamics associated with our losses—always believing that God redeems through ransomed love. Indeed, God covers over what we cover up.

And that is the power of Huldah's prophetic message—to King Josiah, to Judah, and to us today.

HULDAH: "GOD HEARS YOU"

While certainly a coping mechanism for dealing with the raw realities of loss, grief is also a divinely inspired prophetic reminder of the Lord's incarnational presence amidst our pain. Grief is part of God's redemptive, healing work within the brokenness of humanity. The biblical prophets are not just envoys of doom and gloom. They are also ambassadors of grace. Sometimes within the same prophetic message.

Within her seven allotted verses (appearing in both 2 Kgs 22:14–20 and 2 Chr 34:22–28), the prophet Huldah offers both messages. The prophecy of judgment is evident: "Thus says the Lord, I will indeed bring disaster on this place and on its inhabitants—all the words of the book that the king of Judah has read. Because they have abandoned me and have made offerings to other gods, so that they have provoked me to anger with all the work of their hands, therefore my wrath will be kindled against this place, and *it will not be quenched*" (2 Kgs 22:16–17, italics mine). The news is bad. It's the law of sowing and reaping once again convicting the people of Judah of their sins of idolatry and outlaying the devastating punishment that is about to overtake them.

Yet, embedded in her message also was a gift of grace—specifically, for King Josiah, but also meant as a witness to all of us too. Look again at what it says:

> But as to the king of Judah, who sent you to inquire of the Lord, thus shall you say to him, Thus says the Lord, the God of Israel: Regarding the words that you have heard, because your heart was penitent, and you humbled yourself before the Lord, when you heard how I spoke against this place, and against its inhabitants, that they should become a desolation and a curse, and because you have torn your clothes and wept before me, *I also have heard you*, says the Lord. Therefore, I will gather you to your ancestors, and you shall be gathered to your grave in peace; your eyes shall not see all the disaster that I will bring on this place. (2 Kgs 22:18–20, italics mine)

"I also have heard you." God's amazing words of grace were spoken to King Josiah while Josiah was grieving over the sins of his people, repenting for his own complicity with the behaviors of his tribal family, and humbling himself before the Mighty One upon whose mercy he was fully dependent.

God hears us. God hears our lamentation. God hears our prayers—within our own situations of loss and grief, as well as when, like Josiah, like Nehemiah, and like Esther, we take responsibility for the losses caused by the people we are called to lead.

The prophet-leader's role is to walk *into* the darker seasons of life rather than to withdraw from them—knowing that within those shadows of grief-related depression we need not fear, for the rod and staff of our Shepherd are with us (Ps 23:4).

So, in practical terms, how do we do that?

Prophet and Loss

HOW TO NAVIGATE AS A LEADER THROUGH GRIEF-RELATED DEPRESSION

Whether within our personal lives or within the context of our organizations, loss has the capacity to derail our agendas, confuse our emotions, and sabotage our ability to lead—at home or at work. When significant loss pushes us into seasons of depression, it's easy to feel lost, isolated, and alone, questioning our faith, questioning God's plan, and questioning whether God cares or even exists. Grief-related depression in leaders tends to generalize, impacting all facets of life and ministry. Yet there are several strategies to help us navigate through these storms—benefiting both us as well as the organizations that we lead. And all these strategies start with the leaders themselves. These are strategies that invite us into the deeper layers of grief as a spiritual discipline.

Strategy #1: View Depression as a Sign That Healing is Coming

The good news about grief-related depression is that at least we're not in denial, right?! Seriously. It means that we've moved further into the grief mosaic and have begun facing *into* our losses. In other words, grief-related depression is a sign that healing is taking place. To effectively lead—ourselves and our organizations—we must acknowledge the reality of our situation and feel the weight of our loss. Doing so may make us feel completely vulnerable, weak, and out of control, and that is exactly the best place to be when it comes to trusting the God who never wastes a hurt.

Speaking into the challenges facing the Corinthian congregation, the apostle Paul shared about his own struggles with his "thorn in the flesh." In 2 Cor 12:8–10, we read:

> Three times I appealed to the Lord about this, that it would leave me, but he said to me, "My grace is sufficient for you, for power is made perfect in weakness." So, I will boast all the more gladly of my weaknesses, so that the power of Christ may dwell in me. Therefore I am content with weaknesses, insults, hardships, persecutions, and calamities for the sake of Christ; for *whenever I am weak, then I am strong*. (italics mine)

For Paul, weakness was simply "ready soil" into which God's grace would foster deep-rooted growth. Our weakness, God's strength. Do you see the paradox here—the cognitive dissonance that pushes against the typical mindset of a leader?

In 2 Chr 20, as invading armies were encroaching upon the people of Israel in what looked like a no-win scenario, we read that King Jehoshaphat was scared (v. 3) and prayed to the Lord for help. This is how he ended his prayer: "For we are powerless against this great multitude that is coming against us. We do not know what to do, but our eyes are on you" (v. 12). It was within his vulnerability that Jehoshaphat was able to witness the Mighty One of Israel fight his battles.

These are but two examples of the many biblical illustrations showing God as the champion of the weak (Ps 118:7). In Rom 5:1–5, Paul broadens the thesis into a mosaic theological frame:

> Therefore, since we are justified by faith, we have peace with God through our Lord Jesus Christ, through whom we have obtained access to this grace in which we stand; and we boast in our hope of sharing the glory of God. And not only that, but we also boast in our sufferings, knowing that suffering produces endurance, and endurance produces character, and character produces hope, and hope does not disappoint us, because God's love *has been poured into* our hearts through the Holy Spirit that has been given to us. (italics mine)

While this passage is packed with tons of rich theology, for our purposes here, note the perfect tense of *ekkexutai*, "has been poured into." As stated in chapter 1, the perfect tense denotes a *completed* action, the effects of which are continuing into the present. Paul reminds the reader that our sufferings are not the end of our story—or God's. There is a larger mosaic that takes precedence when interpreting the losses and sufferings of God's people.

A mosaic view of our losses helps to position our perspective forward, beyond the scenarios of our pain, toward a God who redeems all things. In God's mosaic, "hope does not disappoint us" (Rom 5:5).

From a faith formation perspective, Janet Hagberg and Robert Guelich argue in their book, *The Critical Journey: Stages in the Life of Faith*, that facing into our losses places us at the critical juncture between what they identify as stage 4 ("the journey inward") and stage 5 ("the journey outward"). For them, it is the paradoxical decision to give up one's search for self-meaning and purpose and instead to surrender in obedience to God's grander plan that brings us peace. Such decisions inevitably require an experience at "the Wall," the pivotal season where, using my language, we grieve the loss of all that has stood in the way of our knowing the full heart of God.[18] Saint John of the Cross would have identified this season as the "dark night of the soul."[19] It is one of the most significantly challenging, confrontational, and personally debilitating seasons a prophet-leader will ever experience. It is also one of the most liberating. And I would argue that it is essential for the formational growth of our capacity to lead—whether it comes at us via hard leadership decisions we've made, or through the sudden death of someone significant in our lives, or in the middle of cardiac rehab.

Strategy #2: Build a Wailing Wall

For grief to be processed in a healthy way, it must be given a "voice." Whether we speak our lamentation out loud, write it within our journals (or books!), draw it with our artwork, or embody it with our lives, our grief needs to find its expression. Otherwise, as with our illustration of the boiling pot in chapter 2, it will come out in other, sometimes more destructive, ways.

We leaders especially must give voice to our pain. We need to be intentional about bringing our losses into our present experience so that we can either respond to them, learn from them, or surrender them to God's healing, redemptive love. Better still, to do all three.

Each of us has a "natural" rhythm of grieving. By "rhythm," I mean a way of grieving that, over time, has been reinforced sufficiently as to become "normal" for us. For example, my natural rhythm is to help everyone else grieve first and then to go off by myself and let go of my emotions. Helping others first has been an avenue for helping me work out my own emotions. There are times, of course, when I'm caught up in the moment with someone and I find myself crying on their shoulder—either for them in their need, or for myself. But generally, my rhythm has been to compartmentalize until a later time. Whether "healthy" (by other's standards) or not, we need to acknowledge what our rhythm is—and then embrace it as a starting point. In fact, plan toward it, rather than fighting it, ignoring it, denying it, or judging it. Regardless of what it is, it's a place to begin.

One of the best ways to do this is for us to develop a "Lamentation Wall," or what I like to call a "Wailing Wall" (giving a shout out to the

---

18. See Hagberg and Guelich, *Critical Journey*, 91–150, for the context and framework for this perspective.

19. See St. John of the Cross, *Dark Night of the Soul*.

Wailing Wall in Jerusalem). Since our losses accumulate over our lifetime, it's helpful to create an inventory of those losses so that we are fully aware of what we are bringing with us into our current experience of grief.

Using a personal journal or sheet of paper, we might begin our inventory by reflecting on the following questions:

1. What are the significant losses that you have experienced over the past year? The past five years? The past fifteen or more years? What losses do you remember from childhood? What feelings do you associate with these memories?

2. Which of these losses has had the most significant impact on you? (You may wish to rate them on a scale of 1 = low impact to 5 = highest impact.)

3. How have these losses defined you (positively and negatively)—in terms of the way you respond to situations, conflicts, personal limitations, risks—both in work/ministry as well as in your marriage/family/friendships?

4. In what ways have you held onto the pain of those losses—for example, by using alcohol, drugs, prescription meds, pornography, or other expressions of "pain management," or through chronic migraines, stomach ailments, muscle spasms, or high blood pressure? Do any of these losses cause you to have nightmares, recurring dreams, or "shadow boxing" thoughts (where you create mental battles in your mind and spar toward a different conclusion for your experience of loss)?

5. How have you allowed (or not allowed) God to "pour out God's love" into your past losses—to redeem them? Which of those losses has caused you to forgive the offender? Which has caused you to withhold forgiveness?

6. On a scale of 1 (not at all) to 10 (extremely high), how would you assess your current level of depression related to these losses?

Writing out our thoughts, or creating another visual representation of our losses, works to inform our unconscious mind and heart that our pain has been "heard." I know that may sound strange to an apostolic leader's way of thinking, but trust me, it works. Giving voice to our pain brings the loss to the present and allows God to bring deeper levels of healing.

This wall can be built organizationally as well. I've done a version of this for a church staff following the completion of a challenging building campaign. I've also done it with one of the seminary spiritual formation classes I cotaught. I've even used this exercise with my own staff and leadership teams while on a strategic planning retreat. It's a wonderful catalyst for moving teams through grief and on toward mission. I've put a sample in the appendix of this book.

Strategy #3: Reevaluate Your Personal Mission-Mandate

Grief is disruptive by nature. It interrupts the normal flow of our work, personal relationships, intimacy, social life, diets, moods, ability to think or reason, capacity to feel emotions—in fact, just about everything. But that's the point. It is designed by God as a process of reorientation. It's an invitation to reevaluate our lives and our priorities and to repolarize ourselves around our True North—God and God's mosaic plan.

As such, losses can be redemptive existentially, assisting us to reevaluate our personal mission mandate—the primary reason we are called to do what we do and to be who we are. Losses provide us with an excuse to call a mulligan, a do-over, if needed. Or they can shake up the Etch a Sketch version of our life so that we may start this next chapter with a clean slate.

So, why not use this season of grief as an opportunity (or excuse) to reevaluate your personal mission mandate and to get help? Have you been living your dream—or dreaming of a better life? Are you constantly shadow boxing with your pain and ending up repeatedly as the victim of your own mental abuse?

Look. Your loss has taken something important from you. Now, I think it's time to demand something from your loss in response. You might want to consider options like these:

1. Get counseling or spiritual direction to work out internal issues of integrity for growth in addition to coping with your grief. While therapeutic, this is not just meant to help you cope with your loss (although that is important), but to engage your loss to see what you may learn or gain from it. My mantra is "God never wastes a hurt, so neither should we."

2. Take a class, a course, or a program to learn new skills. Remake yourself. Increase your leadership capacity. Refuse to be a victim to your own losses. Grieve deeply, but engage life fully.

3. Create a rhythm of reflection—daily, monthly, quarterly, annually. Engage sabbath rest in a new way. Foster opportunities for silence, for worship, for nature walks, or for spiritual journaling. Listen for the Voice of the Holy Spirit speaking into your journey, inviting you into a larger glimpse of God's mosaic plan.

4. Organizationally, begin a strategic planning process (a retreat works well). Ask different questions about the future of your organization—for example, what does God have in mind for our community? What do we have that might help the community? How might our losses have equipped us to help them? Reevaluate your organization's mission and what you need to achieve it. There are wonderful resources out there to do strategic planning. I've also paid to have guest leaders come in and facilitate the process for our teams—giving me the opportunity to be a participant rather than the leader.

Strategy #4: Help Someone Else

The common adage is true: "hurt people hurt people." Many of those who inflict pain on others have been victims of abuse themselves. It's one of the challenging legacies of our times. But I would contend that there's another axiom that is even more true for followers of Jesus: *"hurt people help people."* Grief provides one of the most significant ways for us to learn empathy. Certainly, nobody wants to have to learn empathy that way. It's painful. But it is highly effective—if we trust the process and engage the learning.

To do so, simply choose to help someone else. This act of service breaks the cycle of self-focus and begins to help us engage mosaic living. Acts of kindness disengage us from the mindsets that block forward momentum.

Years ago, one of my younger coworkers came into my office in tears. He had just experienced a very difficult conversation with his supervisor and was feeling extremely judged, misunderstood, devalued, and consequently, ready to quit ministry. After allowing him to vent, I invited him to accompany me on a road trip. I took him with me to visit Lloyd, one of our church members who was in hospice dying from cancer. We spent time reflecting with Lloyd about his life, reading from the Scriptures, sharing communion and prayer, and then leaving to return to the church. On the drive back, I asked my friend how he felt. He replied that helping someone else reoriented his thoughts on what was important. It's been years since that hospice visit, and my friend is not only still in ministry, but he has become a very respected leader within his denomination.

Going through grief ourselves increases our capacity to be better leaders. For those willing to step into the sanctuary of our loss, grief becomes a spiritual discipline that exposes our vulnerability, our fragile mortality, our need for control, our ineffective and photo-shopped facades, and places us at the foot of the cross of Christ, depending on nothing but our Savior's grace. It is there, in that seemingly vacuous space, that we learn to listen. To truly listen.

Developing and using the muscles of empathy tunes our ears to hear the needs of our loved ones, our teammates, our constituents, and our organizations. It gives us the ability to care—not just about the bottom line, but about the people who make that bottom line possible.

As a leader, consider doing the following as a way of processing through your own grief, or as a response to having gone through it:

1. Walk among the people of your organization. Listen to the stories of others and empathize. Seek to understand not just to fix. Listen below what is said: ask yourself, who in my organization (family, staff, team) has been (or might be) impacted negatively by the decisions we're making?

2. Visit someone in hospice. Interview them about their life and what's now important to them.

3. Decide to invest in your community, not just in your product. What are some of the needs of your community? How might your organization—or you personally—help?

Grief's depression is painful. It also can lead us to the cross of Christ where we find our source of hope and new life. Facing into it, we discover that within the dark shadows of our pain, our Savior has kindled a light that beckons us onward. We may not see the full redemptive picture crafted within the mosaic of God's design, but we are invited to catch a glimpse—just enough perhaps to keep us moving forward, toward trusting God with our today and tomorrow.

There, in the trust, we will experience *hesed*—love's unquenchable embrace. Divinely inspired, God's covenantal love has implications for how we are to navigate through the tougher emotions of loss by embodying the mission to which we are called, leading us to acceptance of God's grander mosaic.

For that, we turn now to our next mentor—the prophet Hosea.

A Prophet in Time: Hosea

"Please, Ima! Abba! You're not hearing me! You just don't understand!"

Hosea was pleading with his parents. The children were in bed, finally asleep after an exhausting day. So much had been going on, so much that Hosea was trying to protect them from. Ultimately, he couldn't. He was trying to obtain his parents' support, but they were just not understanding. At least, that's what it felt like.

"Maybe I don't understand either," Hosea said after a pause, exhausted, as he collapsed into a chair at the kitchen table.

"B'ni, we're trying to understand," Hosea's mother, Abigail, began, bordering on being exasperated herself, but using her affectionate "my son" to soften the conversation. She sat down next to her son and put a hand on his arm, more as her way of building a bridge of hope. "But all of what you've been saying, all that you've been through . . . and the children! The *children*! . . . It breaks my heart!"

"Ima, please try to understand." Hosea was talking with his mother, but looking at his father, pleading with him as well. "I know it doesn't make sense. I don't think it does to me either, but I am compelled to do it."

"Compelled?" Beeri spoke for the first time, though his silence for the past hour spoke volumes to his son. They were always close—father and son, working together over the years. Clearly, he loved his son, but these past several years . . . the innocent young child he once knew—he was gone now, somehow replaced with a man who had aged right before his eyes. His once gentle, compassionate spirit had taken on an edge, an intensity that was so unfamiliar to Beeri that it had scared him. Now this son of his was talking crazy. Again.

This entire nightmare had started several years ago. Hosea had been brooding in his room for days. He had gone out into the wilderness the week prior, taking his tent, camping supplies, and a handful of food items from the kitchen cupboards. He had told his mother that he was being "compelled by Adonai to go," and that he would only be gone for a few days at best. It was in that wilderness that Beeri's son changed. When he came home, he stayed in his room for days and would only come out for meals, quickly retreating again, and barely even saying two words to anyone. Something had changed inside of him, Beeri knew it. His son was still there... but different. Very different.

"*Compelled?*" Beeri asked again. "Like before?" He desperately wanted to understand, but mostly he wanted his son back.

"Yes, Abba. Like before." Hosea sounded resigned, but he took that as a sign from his father that he was to continue. "I know it sounds crazy, but I'm supposed to take her back. I *need* to take her back."

"She's a harlot!" fumed Abigail, as she bolted out of her chair, startling the men in the room. "Look at what *that woman* has done to you! Look at how she's abandoned those poor children! I don't want her anywhere near here... anywhere near you or them! No! Absolutely not!"

"Ima, I know. Trust me, I *know*." Hosea's tone was caring, trying to calm his mother's anger, while appreciating how she was defending him. "But Adonai told me to take her back."

"What do you mean, Adonai 'told' you?" Beeri asked.

"Abba... Ima... you better sit down for this."

Hosea had always loved the wilderness. His father had taken him camping there annually since he was a boy—exploring caves and recesses, learning survival skills, camping in the open air when the weather was right. It was during those times that Beeri would tell him the wonderful stories about the heroes of the faith—like Abraham and David. Listening as his father would tell the stories of Moses and the Israelites were his favorite times—how their ancestors were freed from slavery in Egypt by Adonai's mighty hand, how Adonai parted the waters of the great sea, and how Adonai carved out of stone the tablets of the Ten Commandments. In his younger years, Hosea imagined himself as Moses, leading the people through the wilderness and ultimately to the promised land. And for him to hear those stories out in the wilderness made them even more real.

As he grew through his teenage years and now into young adulthood, those wilderness trips took on deeper meaning for him. Several times, Beeri had switched roles, asking Hosea to be the storyteller, giving him the opportunity to embrace his faith heritage personally. Hosea took to that

A Prophet in Time: Hosea

role with great enthusiasm as he recounted the details of each story with only minor corrections from his father.

From those days onward, it was always in the wilderness that Hosea best connected with Adonai. He could hear better out where there were no distractions. He could listen more closely to his soul in the silence provided under the canopy of stars that engulfed his sense of reality. So, it made sense that it would be in the wilderness that Adonai would speak again—this time to Hosea's well-prepared heart.

It had been several years prior that he had begun to hear that Voice inside. It wasn't just in his mind, but deeper, down in his inner being. It was a Voice that was calling him, compelling him to listen, to come to the wilderness again. The Voice was insistent. So, he went. For the first couple of days, he was alone with his thoughts, the Voice being silent. He had only the sounds of the wilderness, sounds that were all too familiar to him—the rock hyrax pups playing near their mother prior to their bedtime, golden jackals howling in the night, and the gentle tapping sounds of deer as they climbed nearby rocks looking for water. Those, plus the crackling of the fire he had built to warm himself in the nighttime temperatures, as well as to ward off any of the more predatory animals in the area, were the sounds underscoring his patient waiting.

But then, on the third night, as he sat by the fire near his tent, the Voice spoke to him. This time much more clearly than ever before. It was the Voice that he connected with the stories that his father had shared. It was the Voice that he had imagined had spoken to Abraham, the Voice Moses had heard at the burning bush—he was sure of it.

It was the Voice that was now speaking to him—the Voice that would now compel him to take on a very different role than what his father had been apprenticing him for. And it would forever change the trajectory of his life.

"*Hosea.*" The Voice began. It was soft, yet distinct, beckoning.

"Adonai?" Hosea whispered, unsure of what to do. Remembering one of his father's stories, he quickly took off his sandals, as he had recalled what Moses had done, and he knelt on the warm sand adjacent to the fire, bowing at the hip and moving his head close to the ground so that his face was resting in the upturned palms of his hands.

"*I AM the God of Abraham and Moses, the God of Joshua and David. I AM the Creator of the stars of the night and the sun that guides you by day.*"

"Adonai!" Hosea exclaimed with a breathless start. He began to shake, every part of his body quaking on the inside in uncontrollable spasms. He was so overwhelmingly scared by the power of the Voice and the palpable presence of the Lord before him that he could not move, could not even open his eyes.

"Hosea ben Beeri, my people, Israel, have prostituted themselves—worshiping other gods. Their infidelity offends me greatly as they have violated our covenant. They have committed adultery, choosing to give themselves to gods of wood and metal, choosing to prostitute themselves with their own greed and lust. Even their priests and prophets—the supposed faith leaders of the community—do not know me or my heart. They are leading the people away from me and the pure faith covenant into which I have called them.[1] They have rebelled against my covenant. They have forsaken me, the One who called them out of Egypt and brought them through the wilderness. Nothing is more important than our covenant. Therefore, judgment is coming on Israel, judgment that is of their own making, and the devastation of which they have not yet seen in all of history."

Hosea was listening intently as the Voice spoke, seeing in his mind's eye the mental pictures of what the Voice was presenting. His heart was breaking with what was breaking Adonai's. He could not imagine what was still to come, for he could not imagine life apart from his first love.

"Hosea, I am sending you *as my messenger. You are to let my people know that judgment is coming. Go, take for yourself a wife of whoredom and have children of whoredom, for the land commits great whoredom by forsaking the Lord.*[2] *Let your life, your very life, be the witness against Israel.*"

It was awkward, for sure, the first time Hosea shared with his parents about his plans to marry Gomer. They didn't really know the full story about her life. In fact, Hosea had not followed the expected path—the path pursued by most young men in that day, a betrothal prearranged by the parents of both bride- and groom-to-be. Gomer's father, Diblaim, was not well-known in Beeri's circles. In fact, he was rather reclusive. Gomer had been rather elusive, too, when asked about her background, so Beeri was unsure how this new arrangement was going to play out.

Yet, Hosea seemed to love her.

The marriage ceremony was rather quick, as was the wedding banquet, by comparison to most in their village. And it seemed that Hosea and

---

1. See Hos 4:4–6.
2. Hos 1:2.

Gomer were also quick with having children—their first, a son, being born within the year after the wedding. Two more would follow successively in subsequent years—a daughter and another son.

What confused Beeri and Abigail most were the names given to these children. A lot of tradition is rooted in a child's name. The typical expectation was to pass on to at least one of the sons the name of the father or grandfather—since their legacy, it was believed, lived on through Adonai's blessings of offspring and the fruit that they would bear.

But that's not what Hosea did. He gave his children rather unique names. To his firstborn son he gave the name Jezreel—an interesting choice, Beeri thought, since it referred to a place of great pain and the slaughter of many innocent lives. To his daughter, he gave the name Lo-ruhamah—which in Hebrew meant "not pitied." To his thirdborn, he gave the name Lo-ammi—which in Hebrew meant "not my people."

It wasn't until after the birth of Lo-ammi that Beeri confronted his son to explain his choice of unique names. It was rather upsetting to him and Abigail to use such negative names when they interacted with their grandchildren. Something was not right, and Beeri needed to know what and why.

"Tell me, b'ni," Beeri asked one evening, as he and Hosea were alone in the kitchen. "Why did you give my grandchildren such . . ." he searched for the right word, ". . . challenging names?"

Hosea paused just as he was about to take a sip from the earthenware cup that his mother had laid out for him before she retired to bed—a drink of milk laced with a bit of honey that had been his nightly ritual since he was five years old.

"Abba . . . can I trust you to not think that I'm crazy?" The question came out haltingly and put Beeri on edge.

"I'm your abba, b'ni. You can tell me anything." The words came out of his mouth, but Beeri wasn't sure he wanted to hear what his son had to say.

"Abba, Adonai told me to do it. Everything I've done, Abba, Adonai told me to do. He spoke to me, Abba. Out in the wilderness. Adonai *spoke* to me!" Hosea recounted all that had happened several years prior, outlining what the Lord had said about the coming judgment and what he, Hosea, was being asked to do. He shared about Gomer's past—and present—indiscretions, and the reasons behind why the Lord had told him to name his children the way he did.

"I know, it sounds crazy!" Hosea whispered. "But it's true. Every word."

Beeri was silent for the longest time, thinking. He was overwhelmed by what Hosea had shared, yet strangely relieved that he now understood what had burdened his son . . . what had changed him.

"I—I believe you." Beeri wasn't sure what to make of the story he had just heard, but he chose to believe that something bigger was happening, bigger than what he was meant to comprehend. Why would he not believe that Adonai was behind this? He certainly understood the accusations that were being made. Israel was not the place it had been when he was a boy. Not anymore. So many had fallen away from the faith. So many were making a mockery of temple worship. Judgment clearly was deserved. Yet, his heart broke for his son.

"Where is Gomer now, b'ni?"

"She's been going out at night." Hearing his own words caused Hosea to cry, tears pouring down his cheeks. "I know that she's being unfaithful to me, Abba. In fact, Lo-ruhamah and Lo-ammi . . . I'm positive that they're not even *my* children. Yet, I love her. And I love them. Truly, I do. I don't know why. It breaks my heart that she wants nothing to do with me. We've tried. Surely, we've tried. It works for a time, and then she disappears again. For several years, it was an ongoing cycle of leaving and then coming back. It's as if she wants to sabotage the best thing she has in her life because she cannot see beyond what she once was."

"What will you do?" Beeri's anger at his daughter-in-law was mastered only by his love for his son.

"Adonai told me that I was to cast her out—as a sign of her infidelity, and as a testimony to the infidelity of Israel." Hosea's words hung in the air between the two men briefly before he continued. "Honestly, she's already embracing another guy. I don't know if she'll even care. But I care. She's the mother of these children . . . *my* children . . . even though she's not been the best example for them."

"You are right to obey Adonai, b'ni. He's got a plan, I'm sure of it."

The story came flooding out of Hosea's mouth, finally leaving him exhausted. The room was now silent. He had shared with his parents that the Lord wanted him to go find Gomer and to bring her back home, to forgive her, and to restore her in marriage and to the family. Hearing the entire story left Abigail speechless. She had so many questions, so many emotions that were stirring inside of her, but she was caught by the intensity, the certainty in her son's eyes. The sandstorm of emotions playing out within her, she was sure, was affecting the children as well. Yet, in that moment, her own maternal instincts drew her upright in her chair.

"Why would you do this? Why?"

"Love redeems, Ima. God's love redeems."

"Go find her then, b'ni. We will make space for her. Adonai, help us—we will make a space for her."

Hosea searched for Gomer for several days, finally finding her by chance. She was standing in a line of women, mostly prostitutes, all of whom were disheveled in appearance. Apparently, they were being auctioned off as slaves. He could only assume that it was to pay off debts or to escape the situation within which they found themselves. Gomer's hair was wild. Her face had multicolored splotches of dried makeup mixed with tears, giving an observer the impression that she had slept in this state for quite a few days. She mostly looked downward, avoiding the gazes of those in the crowd.

Hosea looked at her—broken and debased. And he loved her. Seeing her this way tugged at his heart moving him progressively from anger to pity to compassion to love.

When she was positioned on the auction block and the bidding started, he went to the front of the crowd. He was not leaving there without her. His fee—fifteen shekels of silver and a homer of barley and a measure of wine, the equivalent of thirty shekels of silver,[3] the base price of a female house servant.[4]

Seeing her husband bidding for her brought her to tears. She melted in front of the crowd. She felt deeply ashamed, and yet hopeful for the first time in days, in months even.

They left together—though Gomer walked several paces behind Hosea, her head still low and tears still pouring down her cheeks onto her neck and tattered top. Hosea had made it clear that her restoration would require some time and some specific boundaries[5]—that he needed some evidence of her true repentance before he would reintroduce her to their children.

That night, in prayer, the Voice spoke again.

"Hosea, as with your marriage, so with Israel. Judgment is coming on my people till they turn from their infidelity and return to me. They must get so low that the only response is to look up. And they will surely see me, buying

---

3. Hos 3:2.
4. Exod 21:32.
5. Hos 3:3.

them back. On that day, say to Israel, 'I will make for you a covenant on that day with the wild animals, the birds of the air, and the creeping things of the ground; and I will abolish the bow, the sword, and war from the land; and I will make you lie down in safety. And I will take you for My spouse forever; I will take you for My spouse in righteousness and in justice, in steadfast love, and in mercy. I will take you for My spouse in faithfulness; and you shall know the Lord.'[6] *Indeed, on that day, I will heal Israel's disloyalty; I will love them freely, for My anger will have turned from them."*[7]

Hosea knew that only God's redemptive love could heal the land. He had seen it personally through the parable of his marriage.

And he had to tell his story to Israel—and hope that they would see it too and heed the invitation to repent.

---

6. Hos 2:18–20, modified by me.
7. Hos 14:4, modified by me.

5

Acceptance

To lead our people in fulfilling our mission, we, personally, must become an object lesson of that mission.

For I desire steadfast love and not sacrifice, the knowledge of God rather than burnt-offerings.

—Hosea 6:6

BEING A MISSION-DRIVEN LEADER is hard. Being a mission-driven leader who knows how to navigate through the waves of loss and the emotions of grief connected to their leadership is harder still. It takes a vulnerable leader to lead well—one who has faced into their own losses and is able to let those losses equip their character for the greater plans that God has in store.

Not all leaders are willing. Not all leaders are able. Yet, being vulnerable to the emotional processes of grief is essential for the overall health of the organizations that they lead, and for the well-being—and discipleship—of those who are under their direction.

One of the best ways to view the prophetic witness is by looking at how the biblical prophets represented *with their lives* the messages that God wanted them to deliver.

Whether with broken clay jars and the purchasing of a field (Jer 19:1–12 and 32:6–25, respectively), or with a valley of "dry bones" (Ezek 37:1–28), or by being swallowed by a great fish (Jon 1:17–2:10), God used parables and object lessons to empower the messages of both "doom and gloom," as well as hope and restoration. How Jeremiah, Ezekiel, and Jonah, for example, fared with these real-time object lessons is certainly evidenced by the historical results of their work. Perhaps it's best stated that their prophetic voices were—and are—more impactful with the generations that followed their ministries than within their own time.

Yet, comparatively, I contend that Hosea's "object lesson" required a commitment of significantly greater weight than his prophetic colleagues. To ask a person to do what Hosea had to do clearly goes to the upper limits of what it means to be a leader of God's people, and what it means to trust in God's missional objectives. Was God crossing God's own boundaries to make a point, I wonder?

Certainly, as a side note, it's important to clarify here that the use of the feminine gender within the Hosea storyline in the way both Gomer, specifically, and women, in general, are represented may feel disturbing, even offensive, to the twenty-first-century reader. Yet I reference it within this context to be consistent with the raw, Hebraic hermeneutic present in the prophetic metaphor. It also must be said that regardless of the gender specificity of the storyline and even of the original Hebrew words used, infidelity and faithfulness are each gender inclusive terms, thereby requiring us to see the book of Hosea, within its prophetic and metaphoric presentation, as a truth applying to all of humanity in relation to God.

And that's the point, really. A prophet uses a glimpse of life, a moment in time, to portray a larger mosaic. An object lesson, a parable, a vision, a dream—each captures a part of the grander story that God is creating, and into which God is inviting humanity.

Genuine mission-driven leadership requires such vulnerability, especially as it faces into the grief and losses generated by such leadership—a vulnerability that allows the people of the organization to trust the integrity of the person they are committing to follow.

Simply stated: to lead our people toward fulfilling our mission, *we, personally, must become an object lesson of that mission.*

So, how does one do that? We begin by clarifying the framework of the mosaic by looking at what the prophets saw in part—the central character trait of the Artist who calls us into that mosaic.

HESED AND AGAPE: THE PRIORITY OF LOVE

What Hosea essentially brings to God's mosaic is best expressed by the Hebrew word *hesed*. In Hebrew, *hesed* is faithful, steadfast love. It is unfailing love. It is sacrificial love—when it is given out of a pure motive, a heart for another. It is tangible love—when it is seen in the clear actions of grace shown from one to another. In fact, of its 248 occurrences in the Hebrew Scriptures, it is translated as mercy, kindness, lovingkindness, goodness, kindly, merciful, favor, good, goodliness, and pity.[1] Clearly, it's an important word. I would argue that *hesed* is the central character trait of God, as described in the Hebrew Scriptures. Certainly, there are other character traits that can define the Undefinable One, but *hesed* forms a framework that encompasses them all.

Within our study here, Hos 6:6 becomes the pivotal verse that unpacks the object lesson to which Hosea is called—specifically in Hos 1–3, but also within the judgment-redemption motif embedded in the entire book. When God says through Hosea, "For I desire steadfast love [*hesed*] and not sacrifice, the knowledge of God rather than burnt-offerings," God is indicating to Israel that God wants the same faithful, committed, tangible love *from* them as God has shown *to* them. Such *hesed* is worth more to God than any other act of worship (e.g., temple sacrifices). The intimacy of covenantal love is the greatest picture of the heart of God—and it's what God wants from all of God's people. It has defined the parameters of God's relationship with humanity from the start (see Gen 19:19), even as it filters through the Hebrew Scriptures at regular intervals, especially within the book of Psalms.

By the time we get to the New Testament, the Hebrew concept of *hesed*, as a character trait of God, finds its best expression with the Greek word *agape*. It, too, encompasses the heart and character of sacrificial, tangible, committed, unconditional love—and best describes God's unequivocal love for humanity, as supremely illustrated by the cross of Jesus Christ. John 3:16 clearly and simply catalogues this framework for the entirety of the Gospel: "For God so loved [*agape*] the world that he gave his only Son, so that everyone who believes in him may not perish but may have eternal life." As with *hesed*, *agape* is a choice to put the other before oneself. Here, in John's case, God put the entire world before God's self. In so doing, God, in Jesus, became God's own object lesson to represent the greater mosaic.

---

1. See "חֶסֶד."

Both *hesed* and *agape* express, as best as possible within our human limitations, the heart of God for God's people. Through them we get a glimpse of the ultimate redemptive mosaic that God is designing and into which God is inviting humanity.

THE CALL TO OUT-LOVE THE WORLD

When it comes to leading people through the processes of change and growth, there is an overarching rhythm to an organization's discipling culture that both frames vulnerable integrity and anticipates grief while it invites its participants to harness its energy toward transformation and growth. That rhythm is based on the all-encompassing value of self-giving love—*hesed,* or *agape*. And followers of Jesus are called *to live that love better than the world does.*

When you read the Gospels through the filtering lens of love, you can see by Jesus's interactions with people, including his disciples, just how that kind of love is to be expressed. If we, as followers of Jesus Christ, are to live—and lead by—the values embodied by Jesus, then all we need do is look at what Jesus did and how he interacted with his followers. Jesus apprenticed in love all who chose to follow him. If we watch him closely, he can do the same for us.

As John 13 begins, for example, Jesus is spending his last hours in the Upper Room with his closest friends. He knows what's coming toward him: betrayal, arrest, abandonment, severe beating, a mock trial, scourging, humiliation, crucifixion, and an agonizing death. He knows he has limited time to equip his disciples with what they will need to endure not only the darkest night of their lives, but a mission that will become bigger than they could ever fathom. As an expert carpenter, he has to whittle down all that they saw him do and heard him teach into one main lesson, something they will never forget—an object lesson.

So, Jesus takes off his garments, wraps himself with a servant's towel, grabs a bowl and a pitcher of water from near the entry door, and proceeds to wash his disciples' feet. Each one of them—including the one who would betray him. Despite Peter's protest, Jesus embraces this act of self-denial for it visually implants into each of their memories the profound illustration of that one lesson.

When he finishes, Jesus takes off the towel, puts away the bowl and pitcher, puts his garments back on, returns to his place at the table, and asks

Acceptance

a critically important question: "*Do you understand what I have done for you?*" (John 13:12, italics mine).

I'm thinking that this is one of those "could-hear-a-pin-drop" moments.

Back then, feet were dirty. Literally. And they smelled. Those guys did a lot of walking. Upon entering a home, foot washing was the house servant's job—or the homeowner's, if they could not afford a house servant—as a sign of hospitality. But it also served a very practical purpose: it improved the *atmosphere* of the home. Hold on to that thought.

Jesus's act of humble service demonstrated that genuine love is willing to get dirty. It's willing to shed rights and privilege for the sake of someone else's best. It's willing to assume that another person—any person—is more important than you.

"Do you understand what I have done for you?" the Teacher asks.

Then Jesus explains his object lesson: "You call me Teacher and Lord—and you are right, for that is what I am. So if I, your Lord and Teacher, have washed your feet, you also ought to wash one another's feet. For *I have set you an example*, that you also should do as I have done to you. Very truly, I tell you, servants are not greater than their master, *nor are messengers greater than the one who sent them*. If you know these things, you are blessed if you do them" (John 13:13-17, italics mine).

Within a different context, Matthew's Gospel captures the same leadership lesson from a different perspective—one of sacrificial service. As we saw earlier, in response to a rather bold request from the mother of the Zebedee boys, and then the subsequent bickering of the other ten, Jesus calls them all together and says, "You know that the rulers of the Gentiles lord it over them, and their great ones are tyrants over them. It will not be so among you; but whoever wishes to be great among you *must be your servant*, and whoever wishes to be first among you *must be your slave*; just as the Son of Man came not to be served but to serve, and to give his life a ransom for many" (Matt 20:25-28, italics mine). Within God's grander mosaic, sacrifice is not about giving up something, but rather *giving toward* something—or someone—that is greater than oneself.

In the new community of Jesus followers, typical values are upended, lessons are paradoxical, and disciples are challenged to live—and lead—differently than those in the world. In the new community of Jesus followers, love (*hesed, agape*) is not negotiable.

A NEW COMMAND: LEAD WITH LOVE

Meanwhile, back in the Upper Room Discourse of John's Gospel, in the face of betrayal (Judas, in John 13:18–30) and denial (Peter, in John 13:31–38), both expressions of incredible anticipatory loss, Jesus downloads into them the missional parameters of his object lesson: "A new command I give you: Love [*agape*] one another. As I have loved you, so you must love one another. *By this everyone will know that you are my disciples,* if you love one another" (John 13:34–35, italics mine). Agape love has been demonstrated. And within just a few short chapters—a few short hours beyond that Upper Room gathering—the object lesson would create a seismic impact that would resonate for millennia to come.

I imagine that in that moment with his disciples, as Jesus packages the singular command the way he does, that the anxiety in the room begins to rise. The reality of Jesus's departure was getting more palpable. Judas exits. Peter is confronted with his impending denial. Every impression given to the reader is that Jesus is losing the disciples to their fear. So, he speaks words of peace and promise (John 14) and invites them into a new metaphor, of vine and branches (John 15).

Leadership in the face of loss—perceived or actual—always hits a "crossroads moment" (Jer 6:16) at which time, participants and leaders alike will be invited to make a choice: exit before the pain gets too overwhelming, or stay and go deeper into the harder, character-building challenges of embodying what we say we believe.

Like the master-teacher that he is, Jesus then repeats the main lesson to those remaining:

> As the Father has loved me, so I have loved [*agape*] you; abide in my love. If you keep my commandments, you will abide in my love, just as I have kept my Father's commandments and abide in his love. I have said these things to you so that my joy may be in you, and that your joy may be complete. This is my commandment, that you love one another as I have loved you. No one has greater love than this, *to lay down one's life for one's friends.* You are my friends if you do what I command you. (John 15:9–14, italics mine)

The entire Upper Room Discourse of John 13–17, I would argue, is Jesus's way of equipping the disciples in how to navigate not only through the incredible emotions of grief that they were about to experience, but also in how to empower them to lead beyond their grief into the larger mission to which his death would point. For Jesus, his singular object lesson, further exemplified by his crucifixion, was the most important equipping send-off he could give them. Vulnerable love always makes a way.

LEADING BY A DIFFERENT PRIORITY

While biblical scholars have debated for decades the authorship and cohesiveness of Hos 1–3 with respect to the remaining portions of the prophet's book, personally I believe the beauty of these chapters frames the heart of a God who actively pursues humanity despite our recurrent patterns of infidelity, idolatry, and independent spirit. Without chapters 1–3, the judgment sequences of the rest of Hosea, I contend, are devoid of the intimacy of God's pursuit of *hesed* consistent with the integrity of God's character. These chapters capture an essential quality of leadership that often goes missing both in the corporate world as well as the church—namely, that the leaders *personally* must embody the mission of the organization within the larger mosaic of God's prophetic invitation into vulnerable love, most especially in seasons of loss, when the crossroads decision is before the people.

Love is *the* overarching language of the new community of Jesus followers. Therefore, it must be *the priority* of those of us who lead, regardless of our context of leadership. As leaders, we must model, disciple, reinforce, encourage, and pray for that kind of love within the culture of our organizations. In fact, we must become the object lesson of our mission.

What equips us to do so? In a word, loss.

From Hos 1:1 on, the reader is engaged in a passionate love story between God and an "adulterous" people, where God's faithfulness to a larger mosaic, a mission set in motion centuries prior, supplants even God's own divinely justified feelings of betrayal. God sets aside the full range of judgment to apply undeserved, invitational grace toward a people all because God is committed to a greater purpose.

In God's accountable love for God's "spouse," using the prophetic metaphor of the marriage of Hosea and Gomer, God calls out Israel in their infidelity, naming in truth the evidence of idolatry and adultery in Israel's union with other gods, while also seeing beyond their infidelity toward redemption by the power of God's faithful love. Judgment—and the grief that it inspires—ironically forms a gift of divine grace that leads people into the mosaic of God's healing love.

In God's visionary mosaic, God pours out gracious love, covering over the sins of the people, even renaming Hosea's children (Israel, by proxy) "not my people" to "my people" and "not pitied" to "pitied," and embracing them as part of God's redemptive initiative although, corporately, they still will bear the consequences of their actions.

Prophetic leadership in the face of loss—whether personal or corporate—requires us to embody with our lives the greater mosaic plan of God, a plan that ultimately leads to the cross of Christ, God's redeeming love. The apostle Paul models this for us when, in Phil 3:10, he writes, "I want to know Christ and the power of his resurrection and the sharing of his sufferings *by becoming like him in his death*, if somehow I may attain the resurrection from the dead" (italics mine). Peter, as well, reminds his readers to stay true to the larger mosaic in the face of suffering and loss: "But rejoice in so far as you are sharing Christ's sufferings, so that you may also be glad and shout for joy *when his glory is revealed*" (1 Pet 4:13, italics mine).

In two very practical ways, we embody the mosaic by first, deconstructing the survival mentality of our congregation or organization through bold leadership initiatives, and second, by taking risks that may not make practical sense, but which live out the mission that defines us. Let me share both through the following true story.

EMBODYING THE MOSAIC

Prior to stepping into my role as pastor of Second Street Church in June 2003, I had spent considerable time in prayer asking God to redefine the priorities of my call (see my first book, *Mission Rift*, for more on that process). Those priorities set a course for my leadership since that congregation had been going through a season of conflict that had not only challenged their community identity and purpose, but also depleted many of their financial resources. They had reached a point where the finance team was redirecting monies set aside for missions and outreach to the general operating fund to pay bills. Something had to be done, yet I wasn't exactly sure what. The priorities that the Lord had downloaded into me helped to bolster me in ways I didn't expect.

As I prayed, the Holy Spirit began to confront me on the fact that, for way too long in my life and ministry, I tended to "play it safe." I usually found myself negotiating down the risks connected to ministry to preserve both the church's resources as well as my own reputation. I, too, was in

ACCEPTANCE

survival mode—playing fully into the mainstream survival mentality of most local churches. It was easy to justify such a mode of operation since most finance people were concerned about the bottom line. But the Spirit had something else in mind—something that required me, and us, to deconstruct the survival mode and lead counter to it.

For years, my wife, Kristine, and I would tithe to the local church that we served. It's an ongoing personal commitment of ours that ten percent (or more) of our total gross income would be given to the Lord's work through the general fund of the congregation where we worshiped and served. Any additional giving (e.g., for missions) was above and beyond the tithe. As I started at Second Street, the Spirit impressed on me that the only way out of survival mode was through bold leadership—a partnership of those who are leaders in the church to lead differently together.

For several weeks leading up to the fall's budget session with the finance team, I met with the finance chairperson, Rob, at the time a volunteer in the role. Together, we rebuilt the church's budget, orienting it around a new vision that I was beginning to cast with the congregation. The new budget proposed a three percent *increase* over the prior year, with a commitment to not take resources from the designated mission funds. Rob initially thought I was crazy, but at least on the surface, he humored me. What challenged Rob was the fact that for several years, this church had been seriously divided on multiple levels such that some people who sat on the left side of the sanctuary wouldn't speak to those who sat on the right, even leaving through different exits so as not to run into each other. The finance team reflected those conflicts, he had said, with leaders who had become very controlling over the resources. But we agreed to pray, asking for God's favor over the process.

The evening of the meeting I clearly saw what Rob had referred to—for there was an emotional chill in the room. As the finance team received and reviewed the proposed budget and Rob walked us through the specific changes, I noticed one of the key members, Ken, fold his arms in front of chest and set his jaw on edge. "Three percent increase?" was on the lips of several in the room. Then the room went silent.

"Holy Spirit, guide me," was the prayer that I uttered under my breath as I launched into the silence.

"Friends, I know that three percent seems high given what you all have been through the past couple of years. Yet, I wonder how many of you are pleased with the fact that we've had to take money from missions to pay bills? That tells me that this congregation has been in survival mode. I don't believe God wants any of his churches to be in survival mode, regardless of how many resources might be present. I'm thinking that the way out of our survival mode is by leading—and leading *differently*."

I shared with them that my wife and I believe in tithing—giving a full ten percent of our income to the general fund. And then I said, "Kristine and I really believe in this budget because we really believe that God wants to do something in and through this congregation to impact the surrounding communities for Jesus Christ. We believe in it so much that we, my wife and I, are pledging [and I shared an amount that was larger than our tithe—even scaring me when I said it] to this budget. Now, I don't expect you to give the same amount as us, and I don't expect you to tell this group what you plan to give. But we are leaders at this church and leaders lead. We have no business asking our congregation members to tithe if we ourselves are not willing to do it first. And we have no business making decisions as to how the church is to use its finances if *our* finances are not part of the fund. It's time to lead. So, who's with me?"

Within just a few seconds, Rob said, "I'm in!" Almost immediately afterwards, the chair of our administrative board said, "I'm in!" Of the remaining eight people around the table, about half said, "I'm in too!"

"I KNOW WHAT YOU'RE TRYING TO DO AND IT'S NOT GOING TO WORK"

Just then, Ken looked at me from across the table, arms still folded across his chest, and said, "I know what you're trying to do and it's not going to work."

"Then help me make it work." The words were out of my mouth before I had a chance to think.

At that, something amazing happened. Ken's body language shifted. He released his arms and leaned into the table. He then said, "You're going to have a hard time convincing us older folks to give to a budget that's increasing."

The Spirit seemed to be inspiring me. "Ken," I said, leaning into the table to match his body language, "you know this congregation better than I do. What would *you* do to convince them to join us?"

Ken thought for a moment and then laid out a few key steps that he thought might work.

"Would you be willing to coach me in how to do those steps?" I asked, opening my arms in front of me.

"Yes. Yes, I will."

The rest of the meeting was a blur, but the budget got passed that night. And from that night forward, Ken not only continued to coach me through the many important nuances of leading in that congregation, he became one of my biggest supporters—and closest friends.

By the beginning of 2004, I had my work cut out for me. The new budget included the hiring of a new full-time associate pastor as well as a part-time worship pastor. Things were starting off strong and a new energy could be felt in the congregation. That was when I had my heart attack (see the introduction and chapter 4, if you haven't read them already).

Yet, God revitalized me again with a new mission focus—teach and preach love and forgiveness to reconnect the heart of God's people to God's heart and purpose. So, the finance team and administrative board were about to get yet another challenge.

Teaching love and forgiveness is relatively easy to do from a pulpit or a classroom. The Lord has equipped me to be a good speaker and teacher, so the messages flowed rather easily. And people responded over and over. Truly, the congregation was transforming in ways that could only be attributed to the work of the Holy Spirit. Attitudes were shifting. The leaders were stepping up to their respective roles. The worship attendance was increasing.

A CRAZY IDEA

As fall drew near, Rob and I once again met to lay the course for our budget proposal for the next year. Finances were strong, though giving was still considerably behind the budget needs.

"Rob, I have an idea that you're going to think is crazy."

"Oh?" Rob said, suspiciously.

"I think we need to give away our Christmas Eve offering. And I think we need to give it in ways that meet tangible needs within our community." By this point in our relationship, Rob had already concluded that I was a pastor that pushed the edge on how to do ministry. He didn't shut me down, so I continued. "We began doing this in my former church just before I left. It's an amazing way to show the community that we care, that we're here for them."

Once Rob was on board with the idea, we brought it to the finance team. It took some convincing, but they "tentatively" approved of the concept, saying that we would do it "if we paid all our bills by year's end."

The following week, on a whim, I went to the local police department and talked with the police chief. I told him of our desire to give away our Christmas Eve offering and wondered what needs the police needed in our area. He told me that what they really needed were AED devices, since they are often the first responders to medical emergencies. Each of their six vehicles needed one. That became our target goal.

By the beginning of advent, we were about $40,000 behind in giving, but our leaders wanted to move forward with the plan. I started to communicate with the congregation that we were going to be taking a bold initiative to model what it means to love our neighbors, but would not yet tell them what that plan was.

On Christmas Eve, at each of our services, we shared that we were going to be giving away our entire offering to purchase as many of the needed AED devices as possible and that their generosity was needed.

That night, the Christmas Eve offering was over $12,000—the highest it had ever been. Not only were we able to buy all six AED devices needed, but we had money left over that we then donated to the local fire department toward the purchase of their new apparatus.

And by year's end, the Lord had provided yet another miracle—our deficit disappeared, and we ended the year having paid all our bills, with a surplus besides.

A LIFE CHANGED BY LOVE

Every year since, at that congregation and my next, we have been giving our entire Christmas Eve offering to model love within our neighboring communities.

About ten years after my first encounter with Ken, his wife became seriously ill and passed away. I was privileged to walk with them through that entire process and officiated her funeral at his request. The Sunday after her funeral, Ken was in church for worship. Each week as a routine, we give the congregation an opportunity to fill out "connection cards" with any updates, decisions they are making in faith, or prayer requests. For the first time ever, Ken submitted a card. On it was his name and a single check mark in the box next to, "Today, I give my life to Jesus."

Loss invites us to live out the larger divine mosaic—for it creates a crossroads moment requiring us to trust the One who has called us "out of darkness and into God's marvelous light" (1 Pet 2:9). In the new community of Jesus followers, judgment and grace intersect at the cross of Christ; and divine love, embodied within the relational connections of those who follow Jesus, testifies to the world that we handle grief and loss differently—redemptively, missiologically.

Creating an environment of *hesed* begins, therefore, with us embodying the heart of the One who calls us and sends us to be prophets within the contexts of our organizations—and to do so *because* of the redemptive pain we have experienced within the moments of our own losses.

Epilogue

As an example of suffering and patience, beloved, take the prophets who spoke in the name of the Lord.—James 5:10

Then he took the twelve aside and said to them, "See, we are going up to Jerusalem, and everything that is written about the Son of Man by the prophets will be accomplished." —Luke 18:31

Leaders lead. If we're doing our jobs well, then we're going to be making changes that encourage, empower, and enliven the mission of our congregations and organizations. Inevitably, those changes will require our constituents to adjust their normal rhythms of life to accommodate what is now expected of them. Some of those changes will be received well, and adjustments will be hailed as essential for the benefits yet to come. Some of those changes, however, will not be received well. Our people may react, resist, recoil, and rebel as the ramifications of those changes push them past their comfort zones.

Leaders who have processed well their own personal grief experiences—and perhaps who were willing to face into grief's exacting spiritual discipline—will be equipped better to intuit, hear, interpret, and respond to the denial, anger, bargaining, depression, and acceptance of their people. They will be able to lead with integrity—out of the authenticity of their humanness within the divine mission to which they are called, much like our biblical prophet-mentors.

No loss is "easy" when discerned through the eyes of discipleship. Yet, our losses are the arenas within which genuine spiritual growth occurs. They are the experiences within which the Lord draws us nearer, giving

Epilogue

us an opportunity to glimpse the grander mosaic of God's plan—a plan to prosper and not to harm, a plan to bear greater fruit, a plan to invite, connect, grow, and send God's people into the world to reproduce the love that Jesus demonstrated in his life and on the cross.

Every loss invites us into God's redemptive process of grief, within which we connect our story with God's—if we're willing to engage it.

MY MOM'S MOSAIC

In full transparency, this book was emotionally difficult for me to write—especially the chapters on bargaining and depression. These sections were deeply personal for me, and perfectly timed within my current season of life. As I began writing this book, my mom had been undergoing chemo and radiation for the treatment of stage 3 esophageal cancer. By the time I was ready to start on these two chapters, we had just received the news that, while the original tumors responded well to the treatments and were now gone, the cancer had metastasized to my mom's liver, upping her diagnosis to stage 4. The cancer was aggressive. Treatment, if pursued, would need to be even more aggressive. My dear mother, a strong woman of faith and a highly compassionate retired nurse, made the decision to allow God to do what God had in mind. She decided on no further treatments. The doctor shared that with no treatment, she most likely would have between three to six months to live.

Her initial diagnosis in July of 2022 was truly a surprise, rocking the world of our close-knit family. Just three weeks prior, in total ignorance to what was beginning to consume my mom's insides, my siblings and I, along with our spouses, had gathered at my parents' house for one of our best family reunions. Around their dining room table, we ate, we laughed, we told stories, we ate some more. Three weeks later, we entered a vigil of darkness, searching for rays of hope and healing as we navigated the storm that was upon our family. (I know that many of you reading this right now know exactly the journey I'm describing. You've been there, done that.)

Those rays of hope, indeed, were there too, of course—in the wonderful care that my mom received from the people at the cancer center, in the various people who previously were ministered to by my parents who now came to reciprocate the love, and in the accumulation of small acts of kindness from family, friends, and even total strangers. God was surely present. And God was answering prayers.

Epilogue

Yet we didn't always feel God's presence. And God didn't always answer our prayers the way we wanted. We were needing to trust God in a season when we just wanted God to heal, during a time when we faced circumstances we couldn't change.

Ironically, I was given the unique opportunity to vet all I was writing in this book in real time. Again, and again.

What I've been discovering on this journey is that not only is life precious, so is death: "Precious in the sight of the Lord is the death of his faithful ones" (Ps 116:15). We are people of faith. God's story is bigger than us. Our legacy is not limited to the life that we live. It's also based on the life we leave.

We may leave this life during any of the stages of grief—denial, anger, bargaining, depression, or acceptance. Our personal story can be viewed as a tragedy of accumulated, justifiably painful losses. It can also be seen as a comedy of errors. Or a rom-com (romantic comedy). Or one of the incessantly predictable movies on any one of the typical cable channels. Or it could be viewed as an adventure story—where the hero is redefined, and the villain (since every story seems to have at least one) is not always tangible.

What my mom's journey has been teaching me (notice the perfect tense) is that our glance backward, while significant, is less important than our glimpse forward.

My mom passed away into the arms of her Savior at 11:41 p.m. on April 5th, 2023, yet the hospice nurse officially pronounced her death at 1:10 a.m. on April 6, just after her arrival. April 5 was the beginning of *Pesach*, or Passover. For Jews, Passover reminds them of how God delivered God's people from the bondage of slavery in Egypt—a single event of the past, the effects of which are still experienced today. The centerpiece of that holy feast is the Seder meal, each element of which symbolized a portion of the bitterness of slavery mixed with the prophetic power of their freedom—a freedom bought at great price. April 6, 2023, was Maundy Thursday—a time for Christians to remember Jesus's last hours with his disciples, last commands to those who would follow him, and final acts of self-sacrifice that would propel them onward in the mission of God. The centerpiece of this holy day is another Seder meal, what we know as the Last Supper, yet another gathering around the prophetic table to remember together the suffering and death of Jesus, and the freedom that was bought at a great price—until Jesus comes again in final victory.

EPILOGUE

My mom's death spanned the markers of two perfect-tense events in time, while it also created yet a new one for me and for my family. Certainly, we are forever changed by her death. More so, we have been forever changed by her life. Our stories and God's story intersect again, forming yet another crossroads moment demanding a response.

God's mosaic beckons us.

AN ANCIENT PATH

Jeremiah, Anna, Hannah, Huldah, Hosea. They all came to understand. Any view behind them was to propel the people forward. Each in their own way, they invited the people to "stand at the crossroads, and look, and ask for the ancient paths, where the good way lies; and walk in it, and find rest for [their] souls" (Jer 6:16). Their messages of judgment were also messages of grace—clouded, for sure, by the pain and grief that accompanied their tough-love-accountability, but grace, nonetheless. They were envoys of Almighty God, sent with the prophetic word of hope, albeit many times fully digested in the reflux acid of unrequited love (Rev 10:9–10).

Mosaic-thinking is not a new concept. Prophet-leaders have been engaging it since biblical times. Facing his own litany of losses, Job portrays a glimpse of the mosaic: "For I know that my Redeemer lives, and that at the last he will stand upon the earth" (Job 19:25).

The apostle Paul saw it as well. In Phil 3:7–16, he wrote:

> Yet whatever gains I had, these I have come to regard as loss because of Christ. More than that, I regard everything as loss because of the surpassing value of knowing Christ Jesus my Lord. For his sake I have suffered the loss of all things, and I regard them as rubbish, in order that I may gain Christ and be found in him, not having a righteousness of my own that comes from the law, but one that comes through faith in Christ, the righteousness from God based on faith. I want to know Christ and the power of his resurrection and the sharing of his sufferings by becoming like him in his death, if somehow I may attain the resurrection from the dead. Not that I have already obtained this or have already reached the goal; but I press on to make it my own, because Christ Jesus has made me his own. Beloved, I do not consider that I have made it my own; but this one thing I do: forgetting what lies behind and straining forward to what lies ahead, I press on towards the goal for the prize of the heavenly call of God in Christ Jesus. Let those

of us then who are mature be of the same mind; and if you think differently about anything, this too God will reveal to you. Only let us hold fast to what we have attained.

When you look death in the face and you see faith looking back, you know you're standing on holy ground.

Perhaps that is our greatest legacy—simply to live a life that has held onto Jesus. Only Jesus. In doing so, both prophet and loss find their truest Voice, deepest meaning, and greatest hope.

Appendix:
Building a Mosaic—A Group Exercise

For groups of eight or more, try this exercise. You will need four sets of different colored 4 x 6 (or larger) index cards. Half-sheets of 8½ x 11 colored paper work great too. You will need one set of cards for each participant, each set consisting of one of each color. Each color will correspond to one of the questions below. You will also need a marker for each participant, black or dark blue so responses will be readable on the color cards/sheets; several rolls of masking or regular tape to attach the cards/sheets to the wall; and a large wall space in your meeting area. With the materials handed out to the participants, the leader begins the exercise with the following instructions:

"A mosaic is an ancient art form that consists of individually painted or decorated tiles that, when put together, create a picture or design. That picture or design is then best viewed from a distance. Our job today is to build a mosaic that represents our past year (season, project).

"In reflecting over the past year (season, project), I'm going to ask a series of questions. I'd like for you to answer the questions honestly and write your answers on the card/sheet. I'll tell you which color goes with each question. I'm going to ask you to share your answers with the group, but I realize that not all participants will feel comfortable doing so. Please consider it, but know that I'm not going to make you do what you're not comfortable doing. After the group has responded to each question, I'll ask that you take your colored card/sheet and tape it randomly on the designated wall space. It can go anyway you'd like in the designated area. We'll do this process after each question. Together, we are going to build a mosaic wall."

Appendix: Building a Mosaic—A Group Exercise

1. Affirmation Wall (pick a color card/sheet)—Who on my team am I proud of and why? (It can even be yourself.)
2. Lamentation Wall (pick a different color card/sheet)—What's one thing I need to let go of in order to move forward? (Or what's one thing I'm afraid will happen as we move forward?)
3. Celebration Wall (pick a different color card/sheet)—Depending on the situation...
   a. What's one thing my team, my ministry area, the staff team, or the leadership accomplished that needs to be celebrated?
   b. Or... what's one thing in my life that I'd like to celebrate?
4. Prayer Wall (pick a different color card/sheet)—What's one thing I need from God as we move forward?

Ask each question one at a time giving ample time for participants to write a word, name, phrase, or statement on the corresponding question's color card/sheet. Then, going around the room, invite people to share out loud their responses. After all have shared their answers to that question, as a group, invite them to go up to the wall and randomly place their individual cards/sheets on the wall space.

Repeat the process with each successive question using a different color card/sheet.

When all questions are completed and the cards/sheets are all on the wall, invite the group to look at the "mosaic" that was created. Ask the group to gather close to the wall and to read the various cards. Ask them to step back several paces and to now look at the way the colored cards form a mosaic. Ask them: "What do you observe about the mosaic?" (e.g., "We tended to group the same colors together rather than spreading them out," "There seems to be more lamentation cards than affirmation ones"). If appropriate, end the session with a group circle prayer—offering thanksgiving for the affirmations and celebrations, and praying for the hurts, heartaches, and concerns. Have the group informally share how the experience made them feel, what they learned about themselves or about the team.

Works Consulted

Amatenstein, Sherry. "The Dilemma of High-Functioning Depression." Psycom, Nov 8, 2022. https://www.psycom.net/depression/high-functioning-depression.

Augsburger, David. *Caring Enough to Forgive*. Scottsdale, PA: Regal, 1981.

———. *Helping People Forgive*. Louisville: Westminster John Knox, 1996.

Bair, Alisa. *Grief is a Dancer: A Memoir*. Lancaster, PA: Walnut Street, 2021

———. *A Table for Two: A Mother and Her Young Daughter Face Death Together*. Intercourse, PA: Good Books, 1998.

Berra, Lodovico. "Existential Depression: A Nonpathological and Philosophical-Existential Approach." *Journal of Humanistic Psychology* 61.5 (March 2019) 757–65. https://journals.sagepub.com/doi/10.1177/0022167819834747.

Blair, Anthony, et al. "Prophets, Priests, and Kings: Re-Imagining Ancient Metaphors of Diffused Leadership for the Twenty-First Century Organization." *Journal of Management, Spirituality and Religion* 9 (2012) 127–145. https://www.ingentaconnect.com/content/jmsr/rmsr20/2012/00000009/00000002/art00002;jsessionid=46nn6kbkuie3d.x-ic-live-03.

Bonhoeffer, Dietrich. *The Cost of Discipleship*. New York: Macmillan, 1963.

Bridges, William, and Susan Bridges. *Managing Transitions: Making the Most of Change*. 4th ed. New York: Hachette, 2016.

Cassata, Cathy. "What is Existential Depression?" PsychCentral, May 26, 2021. https://psychcentral.com/depression/what-is-existential-depression.

Cloud, Henry. *Necessary Endings: The Employees, Businesses, and Relationships That All of Us Have to Give Up in Order to Move Forward*. New York: Harper Business, 2010.

Coleman, Peter T., and Robert Ferguson. *Making Conflict Work: Harnessing the Power of Disagreement*. Boston: Mariner, 2015. Kindle ed.

Crosby, Henry Lamar, and John Nevin Schaeffer. *An Introduction to Greek*. Boston: Allyn and Bacon, 1928.

Dean, Kenda Creasy, and Ron Foster. *The Godbearing Life: The Art of Soul Tending for Youth Ministry*. Nashville: Upper Room, 1998.

"Decompensation." APA Dictionary of Psychology. https://dictionary.apa.org/decompensation.

DiChiara, Tom. "Is the 'Runner's Wall' a Real Thing?" WebMD. https://www.webmd.com/fitness-exercise/features/is-the-runners-wall-a-real-thing.

"DiSC Styles." DiSC Profile. https://www.discprofile.com/what-is-disc/disc-styles.

"Dunamis," Bible Tootles. https://www.bibletools.org/index.cfm/fuseaction/Lexicon.show/ID/G1411/dunamis.htm.

Works Consulted

Enago Academy. "'If-Then': Using Conditional Sentences in Academic Writing." Enago Academy, Nov 15, 2021. https://www.enago.com/academy/ifthen-using-conditional-sentences-in-academic-writing/.

Enright, Robert. "Psychological Science of Forgiveness: Implications for Psychotherapy and Education." Paper presented at the Conference, Neuroscience and Moral Action: Neurological Conditions of Affectivity, Decisions, and Virtue, Rome, Italy, February 2011. https://www.academia.edu/56539157/Psychological_Science_of_Forgiveness_Implications_for_Psychotherapy_and_Education.

Fife, Stephen T., et al. "Facilitating Forgiveness in the Treatment of Infidelity: An Interpersonal Model." *Journal Of Family Therapy* 35.4 (2013) 343–67.

Frankel, Lois P. "Depressed Organizations: Identifying the Symptoms and Overcoming the Causes." *Employment Relations Today* 18.4 (Winter 1991) 443–51. https://onlinelibrary.wiley.com/doi/10.1002/ert.3910180407.

Friedman, Edwin H. *A Failure of Nerve: Leadership in the Age of the Quick Fix*. New York: Church, 2017.

Frise, Nathan R., and Mark R. McMinn. "Forgiveness and Reconciliation: The Differing Perspectives of Psychologists and Christian Theologians." *Journal of Psychology and Theology* 38.2 (2010) 83–90.

Gajdos, Kathleen Curzie. "The Intergenerational Effects of Grief and Trauma." *Illness, Crisis and Loss* 10.4 (October 2002) 304–17. https://journals.sagepub.com/doi/10.1177/105413702236514.

Gauger, Robert W. "Understanding the Internal, External, and Spiritual Factors of Stress and Depression in Clergy Serving the Southside of Jacksonville, Florida." DMin diss., Regent University, 2012. https://www.proquest.com/docview/1040723092?pq-origsite=gscholar&fromopenview=true&sourcetype=Dissertations%20&%20Theses.

Gault, Ann, ed. "The Five Stages of Grief: An Examination of the Kubler-Ross Model." Psycom, Jun 7, 2022. https://www.psycom.net/stages-of-grief.

Gill, Jesse. *Face to Face: Seven Keys to a Secure Marriage*. Bloomington: WestBow, 2015.

Griffin, Brandon J., et al. "On Earth as It Is in Heaven: Healing through Forgiveness." *Journal Of Psychology and Theology* 42.3 (2014) 252–59.

Hagberg, Janet O., and Robert A. Guelich. *The Critical Journey: Stages in the Life of Faith*. Salem, WI: Sheffield, 2005.

"חֶסֶד." Blue Letter Bible. https://www.blueletterbible.org/lexicon/h2617/kjv/wlc/0-1/.

Jackson, Michael. "Reconnecting the Rhetoric and Reality of Forgiving and Remembering." In *Forgiving and Remembering in Northern Ireland: Approaches to Conflict Resolution*, edited by Graham Spencer, 41–59. London: Continuum International, 2011.

Jeffreys, J. Shep. *Helping Grieving People—When Tears Are Not Enough: A Handbook for Care Providers*. 2nd ed. New York: Routledge, 2011.

Johnson, Susan. *Attachment Theory in Practice: Emotionally Focused Therapy (EFT) with Individuals, Couples, and Families*. New York: Guilford, 2019.

———. *Emotionally Focused Couple Therapy with Trauma Survivors: Strengthening Attachment Bonds*. New York: Guilford, 2005.

Knopf, Eric. "Learn about the Fivefold Ministry." Five Fold Ministry. https://fivefoldministry.com/pages/learn-about-the-fivefold-ministry.

Kübler-Ross, Elisabeth. *Death: The Final Stage of Growth*. New York: Touchstone, 1975.

———. *On Death and Dying: What the Dying Have to Teach Doctors, Nurses, Clergy and Their Own Families*. New York: Scribner, 1969.

Works Consulted

Kübler-Ross, Elisabeth, and David Kessler. *On Grief and Grieving: Finding the Meaning of Grief through the Five Stages of Loss*. New York: Scribner, 2005.

Lares, Andres. "The Most Important Rules of Negotiation." Shapiro Negotiations Institute, Mar 18, 2021. https://www.shapironegotiations.com/the-most-important-rules-of-negotiation/.

Magnuson, Chad M., and Robert Enright. "The Church as Forgiving Community: An Initial Model." *Journal of Psychology and Theology* 36.2 (2008) 114–23.

Marty, Martin E. "The Ethos of Christian Forgiveness." In *Dimensions of Forgiveness: Psychological Research and Theological Perspectives*, edited by Everett L. Worthington, 9–28. Radnor, PA: Templeton Foundation, 1998.

McConville, J. Gordon. "Forgiveness as Private and Public Act: A Reading of the Biblical Joseph Narrative." *Catholic Biblical Quarterly* 75.4 (2013) 635–48.

McMinn, M. R., et al. "Forgiveness and Prayer." *Journal Of Psychology and Christianity* 27.2 (2008) 101–9.

Menahem, Sam, and Melanie Love. "Forgiveness in Psychotherapy: The Key to Healing." *Journal Of Clinical Psychology* 69.8 (2013) 829–35.

Moeller, Stephen. "Transgenerational Grief." The Grief Recovery Method, Jan 9, 2018. https://www.griefrecoverymethod.com/blog/2018/01/transgenerational-grief.

"Mosaic." Merriam-Webster. https://www.merriam-webster.com/dictionary/mosaic.

Murray, Robert J. "The Therapeutic Use of Forgiveness in Healing Intergenerational Pain." *Counseling and Values* 46.3 (2002) 188–98.

Myers, Ched. "Jesus' New Economy of Grace: The Biblical Vision of Sabbath Economics." *Sojourners* (1998). https://sojo.net/magazine/july-august-1998/jesus-new-economy-grace.

Patton, John. *Is Human Forgiveness Possible? A Pastoral Care Perspective*. Lima, OH: Academic Renewal, 2003.

Puls, Darrell. *The Road Home: A Guided Journey to Church Forgiveness and Reconciliation*. Eugene, OR: Cascade, 2013.

Reeve, Jim. *God Never Wastes a Hurt*. Lake Mary, FL: Creation House, 2000.

Roberts, Terri, and Jeanette Windle. *Forgiven: The Amish School Shooting, a Mother's Love, and a Story of Remarkable Grace*. Minneapolis: Bethany House, 2015.

Ross, Lee, and Richard E. Nisbett. *The Person and the Situation: Perspectives of Social Psychology*. 2nd ed. London: Pinter and Martin, 2011.

Rye, Mark S., et al. "Religious Perspectives on Forgiveness." In *Forgiveness: Theory, Research, and Practice*, edited by Michael E. McCullough et al., 17–40. New York: Guilford, 2001.

Segal, Sara Chana. "When the Grief You Are Carrying Is Not Your Own." Integrative Psychotherapy. https://integrativepsych.co/new-blog/intergenerational-grief.

Shaw, Michael C. *Faithful Are the Wounds: A Memoir*. Maitland, FL: Xulon, 2023.

Solomon, Yoram. "10 Rules that will Help You Win Negotiations." *Inc.*, Jan 17, 2017. https://www.inc.com/yoram-solomon/10-rules-that-will-help-you-win-negotiations.html.

St. John of the Cross. *Dark Night of the Soul*. Critical edition of P. Silverio de Santa Teresa, C.D. Translated by E. Allison Peers. Mineola, NY: Dover Publications, 2003.

"Sublimation." *Psychology Today*. https://www.psychologytoday.com/us/basics/sublimation.

"Subversion." Cambridge Dictionary. https://dictionary.cambridge.org/us/dictionary/english/subversion.

Thurman, Howard. *Jesus and the Disinherited*. Boston: Beacon, 1976.

Works Consulted

United Methodist Church. "A Service of Word and Table I." In *United Methodist Book of Worship*, 6–11. Nashville: United Methodist, 1992.

Van der Kolk, Bessel. *The Body Keeps the Score: Brain, Mind, and Body in the Healing of Trauma*. New York: Penguin, 2014. Kindle ed.

Woolverton, David. *Mission Rift: Leading through Church Conflict*. Minneapolis: Fortress, 2021.

www.ingramcontent.com/pod-product-compliance
Lightning Source LLC
Chambersburg PA
CBHW062043220426
43662CB00010B/1632